From Achill Island to Zennor

From Achill Island to Zennor

*Adventures of an intrepid traveller
to the extremes of the British Isles*

JOHN DAVIES

FIRST EDITION

ISBNs
eBook: 978-1-80227-801-9
Paperback: 978-1-80227-800-2

Prepared and typeset by *PublishingPush.com*

To Josiane

Thank you again for inspiring me to write my second travel book

JOHN DAVIES

The author outside Pembroke Castle in 2018

John was born in Neath, South Wales, in 1943. He had a varied and extensive career on the railways, spanning 33 years and commencing in 1961. It started after he left Neath Grammar School with a distinction in Geography for his A-Level studies. John's railway experience covered both freight and passenger sectors with a strong emphasis on marketing, ultimately culminating in his position as Regional Railways Manager for Wales. After taking early retirement, John continued working as an independent transport consultant and subsequently set up a partnership – BayTrans – promoting sustainable travel for visitors to Swansea Bay – a very successful venture that he is still pursuing well beyond retirement age!

John's lifelong passion for travel carried him around the British Isles, Europe, and North America. His interests were shaped by his love of geography, the natural world, and transportation in all its forms.

John married Josiane in 1995. A Parisian, Josiane has been both the inspiration and the impetus for this second book of his.

November 2022

ACKNOWLEDGEMENTS

First is the debt I owe to my wife Josiane, who encouraged me to write a second book. Following the success of 'From Hell to Paradise and a thousand places in between' about my adventurous travels in Europe and North America, she insists there must be a similar story to tell about my even greater number of journeys in my own country.

Second, I wish to acknowledge close friends who accompanied me on my trips between the 1960s and 1993; since that year, Josiane has been my companion on many of my journeys. I have permission to use their names (in the text as first names only), and there are a few who I cannot get in touch with:

Brian Thompson, Edward Porter, Hugh James, Paul Collenette, Peter Duncan, Peter Griffiths and Robert Thomas. Brian Williams sadly is no longer with us, and I've lost touch with David Smythe and Trevor Davies

To Professor Stuart Cole, long-time friend, and colleague, for putting together such a fine foreword.

To Colin Speakman, author and sustainable transport campaigner, for advice and help on the way.

To Nathalie Thomas and Isabelle Thomas for assistance with text, layout and design.

To Publishing Push for their help in taking this book to market.

Photographs:

Most photographs are by the author. Other photographs and images are taken from various sources and are appropriately acknowledged.

Cover images: front is Slieve Leagues in County Donegal, Ireland (Brholden-public domain); back is Exford village in Exmoor National Park (author) and the train image is on the Lynton & Barnstaple Heritage Railway (author).

Contents

Foreword

Achill Island to Zennor is a very personal journey record by an author who made his living – and who, to me – will always be associated with railways. But John Davies' book is multi-modal, covering train, bus, foot, cycle, car, and air travel.

This book shows how John travelled to the island nations of Wales, Scotland, England, and the Emerald Isle of Ireland. However, it isn't just a travel book. It is more a reflection of a very human personality which is John.

He uses an interesting research methodology and one I would not have expected in the thirty years I've known him. I would not have seen this respectable railway 'servant' as a law breaker searching material – with his first pint at 16 – and hiding from a train inspector on an unofficial freight train ride!

Indeed, he was the first British Rail Manager for Wales and the forerunner of the Wales and Borders franchise. John gave evidence to the House of Commons Select Committee on Welsh Affairs (1991) when I served as an adviser to the Committee's transport inquiries. In such high regard, he was (and is) held.

This book combines historic transport modes between the 1950s and 2010s with scenes of the most stunning parts of these islands, whose descriptions are so captivating; *Visit Wales* could do well to make use of them. Fortunately for the reader, he kept detailed accounts of his trips and important high-definition photographs of the locations.

Travellers' tales are snappy and, like the rest of the book, have an easy reading style, and John's enthusiasm really comes through. I loved the 'train jam' at Machynlleth and John's 'political' performance, giving a presentation without believing a word of it!

An affinity with many of the places and routes described by John brought back a favourite *Iarnrod Eireann* train journey; from Dublin Heuston to Limerick Junction (with the bizarre change for Limerick), enriched with a large steak and chips watered down with several Guinness' on a Mark 2 coach. Also recalled were many rail journeys all over these islands: in Wales (where I have lived and worked), Ireland (holidayed and worked), East Anglia (university, the 1960s, and the operation of *'Lodekka'* and *'K-type'* buses).

We are reminded of historic operations with trains detaching and attaching carriages to/from London trains at intermediate stations, the weekly ticket, which, if reintroduced, would serve today's sustainable travel market and increase patronage, and Moat Lane Junction and associated lines which allowed north-south travel entirely within Wales.

Much of the book is anecdotal, and all the better for those tales of John's travel adventures that make the journeys so colourful. Visiting the places in *Achill Island to Zennor* just to see the changes would also be a travel guide with a difference.

Professor Stuart Cole CBE
Emeritus Professor of Transport, University of South Wales

To begin at the beginning (Dylan Thomas); many of my British journeys started out around Swansea Bay.

Welcome to this, my second travel Odyssey; having transported my readers to exciting and exotic places in Europe and North America in the first book, my wife Josiane suggested I have an even bigger story to tell about travels in my homeland. But it's a greater challenge owing to the sheer number of journeys and places I have visited in Great Britain and Ireland. Taking both rail and road trips, I've travelled over a million miles in these islands and climbed a further twenty vertical miles in my mountain adventures.

For this book is a celebration of my reaching the outermost ends of these islands and some of their greatest heights, and of the adventures that go with this achievement. As well as describing some of my exotic train journeys, I look at the general transport scene over the years, celebrate the wonderful landscapes and seascapes along the way, and finally, talk about people and events to add a bit more spice.

As before, much of my narrative is written in the present tense as this will evoke a feeling of 'being there' whether on a train journey or at the summit of a great mountain.

The title well represents an A to Z of places where I've been: my A – is Achill Island in the far north-west of the Irish Republic – as remote and exotic as you can get and my Z – is Zennor (the only Z I know of) in the far southwest of England, which I see from the top deck of an open-top bus from St Ives to Penzance in Cornwall. One of my travel adventures may be unique. I wonder how many – if any – others have journeyed between South and North Wales by *six* different travel modes (from foot to air). Or have experienced an adventure like mine in the Republic, stowing away on a freight train close to the border with Northern Ireland a year before 'The Troubles.' And being present at the 'piping off' Britain's very first Scottish Nationalist MP on to the overnight *Loch Seaforth* from Stornoway, Lewis, to arrive in Westminster 48 hours later. Finally, the climbing of Britain's highest and one of its lowest peaks.

There is more about trains and train travel in this book, and though these journeys may not be as exotic as others I have done in Europe or North America, you will discover many fascinating experiences, not only on the longer journeys. As the railways don't generally extend to the extremes of our nations, I have sought many other means (ship, bus, walking) to get me to iconic places.

With so much to choose from, I have been very selective and make no apology for confining my experiences to places and regions I particularly like, so Wales naturally gets a good look in. Otherwise, both Scotland and Ireland give me much interest to write about train journeys and scenic splendours whilst in England, much of my narrative is in the West Country and the North of England as two parts of the country which I not only like but have strong associations with whether for business or pleasure. And that has also led me to write about the three interesting English cities I have lived and worked in.

Finally, I have a story to tell about my love of the outdoors, especially the mountains as these form parts of my travel adventures done at a more leisurely but often strenuous pace. Many will have bagged more *'Munro's'* than I, but I pride myself on having tackled a cross section of mountains in various parts of Scotland, Wales, and England, thereby seeing the landscape from a totally different perspective.

My early journeys in the British Isles were often made with close friends, and some were done solo. Unlike in Europe and North America, I do not make many long journeys by train with my wife Josiane after our marriage in 1995 though we have a lot of trips around Wales in pursuit of various consultancy engagements and our long-distance holidays in the West Country, the Lake District, Yorkshire, and various English cities.

Footnote: In the ensuing text are a number of technical, colloquial, or other expressions not in general use or knowledge. To assist the reader, a glossary of such terms is provided at the end of this book.

Josiane and John

Between South and North – Six Ways: Walk > Cycle > Car > Bus > Train> Plane

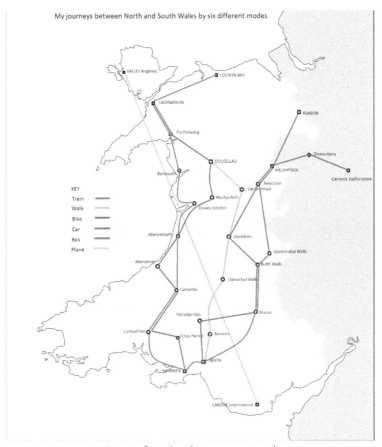

Map of Wales (maproom.net)

I'm a prolific traveller, a trait my father instilled in me from an early age. Family travel tends to be to distant places for the summer holidays. In 1953 it is Colwyn Bay in North Wales and is the first of many train trips and first by any travel mode across the whole of Wales. My second visit to the north in 1960 is on foot; my geography teacher Owen Thomas challenges his sixth form students to learn about Wales from the ground! Later that year, I cycle through much of Wales with a friend who has moved to Staffordshire, and we travel from there to Neath via Welshpool and Brecon. It's 5 years on to my first car journey in a friend's Ford Anglia from Neath to Ruabon in 1965 for a Scouts Jamboree. My bus journey is in 1999 when I take *Traws Cambria* from Swansea to Caernarfon. Five down, one to go, and who could have thought of flying by scheduled service? My sixth and final mode is in a small turbo-prop plane from Cardiff to Valley on Anglesey in 2007. Beat that!!

My Great Welsh Train Journey | August 1953 Neath to Colwyn Bay

In the summer of 1962, the southbound Butlin's train is ready to leave Aberystwyth.

It is 1953 and I am ten years old and about to set off on the train journey of a lifetime; from 1964, this route is no longer a viable travel option with the closure of the Carmarthen-Aberystwyth and Afon Wen-Caernarfon lines, though the highly scenic Cambrian Coast Line is still there. 1953 is the first year that a through train runs on Saturdays in the summer for visitors to *Butlin's* at Pwllheli. As an experimental service, it starts from Carmarthen and terminates at Penychain, the station for *Butlin's* camp. A year later, it becomes a regular summer train from Swansea to Pwllheli over the same route. Perversely, a non-corridor train of eight coaches is provided, and consequently, with frequent 'toilet' stops en route! This, and that it is hauled throughout by small locomotives, means that it inevitably loses a lot of time.

It departs Carmarthen at around 11:00, hauled by an ex-GWR '2251' class locomotive, and takes the line north to Aberystwyth, 56 miles which normal service trains are scheduled to do in two and a half hours, at an average speed of 25 mph. Our train takes longer due to the unscheduled stops for the 'relief' of passengers. It's a scenic run through Carmarthenshire and Cardiganshire; approaching Aberystwyth, the line describes an 'arc,' and the sea suddenly comes into view as we cross over the narrow-gauge 'Vale of Rheidol' line. The train reverses at Aberystwyth, where another locomotive, an ex-Cambrian Railways type, one of a few still in service, takes it to Dovey Junction, where we reverse again. Time is going on though this is of little concern to me; enjoying every minute of the trip. From Dovey Junction, now on the famous Cambrian Coast Line, we have a BR Standard Class 2 locomotive.

A BR Standard Class 2 on a freight train at Porthmadog in 1962.

In the summer of 1963, a Pwllheli to Manchester train approaches Afon Wen.

These handsome locomotives are suited to low axle-load routes like the Cambrian. The journey is a joy, and the coastal scenery backed by mountains is out of this world! The highlight of the trip is the iconic viaduct over the Mawddach estuary with *Cader Idris* dominating. This journey is to end at Penychain, the station for *Butlin's,* and passes non-stop through Afon Wen, a junction for the Bangor line, so we double back on a one-coach shuttle hauled by another BR Standard Class 2. There, we transfer from Western to London Midland Region, taking a local train to Bangor and hauled by an ex-LMS Class 4 tank locomotive. This line is heavily used in the summer by *Butlin's* specials from Manchester. En route, it calls at Caernarfon where we get a good view of its famous castle. Bangor is our final change of trains as we take a local bound for Chester, hauled by an ex-LMS 'Black 5' to Colwyn Bay, where arrival is after 21:00. It is quite some trip and one I will always remember.

A wonderful holiday ensues, including a train trip to Blaenau Ffestiniog in an observation car. We spend the intermediate Saturday at lineside watching a continuous procession of holiday trains all day. During the week, we take a short ride on the *Welsh Dragon*, Britain's only named local train, to Llandudno and ride back on the amazing Llandudno-Colwyn Bay tram.

The unique *Welsh Dragon* named train at Colwyn Bay in 1962.

My Great Welsh Walk · Easter 1960 Neath to Dolgellau

En route at Abergwesyn, Keith, Gareth, self, and Jeffrey pose for our teacher.

At the start of the 1960s Easter holiday, four sixth formers from Neath Grammar School set out on what turns out to be a 115-mile walk over eight days between Neath and Dolgellau in Gwynedd. The motivation for the walk is a challenge from our geography teacher, Owen Thomas, that the best way to learn the geography of Wales will be to walk through it. The challenge is accepted, and three teams of four set off for Snowdonia. I don't recall if the other two teams made it all the way.

We meet at Neath Grammar School and start by walking along the main road to Aberdulais, turning onto the extant Sarn Helen, a Roman road stretch. In typical Roman fashion, this takes a mainly straight trajectory along the mountain ridge between the Neath and Dulais Valleys, a long and boring march, as I recall. We come off the mountain at Banwen and to the first pub on the walk, the Pantyddrainen Hotel. Here I learn the art of blackmail. We are all 16 and thus under-age, but it seems I look a bit younger than the other three, and the barmaid agrees to serve pints to them but not to me. While she is drawing the beer, I nudge them, "Do I tell her we are all the same age, or do you tell her I'm the same age as you?" I get my pint of beer!

From here, we walk along the Roman road for another mile towards Coelbren, then take a minor road into the Swansea Valley, along the A4067 Brecon Road to our campsite for the night, located very conveniently opposite the Gwyn Arms in Craig-y-Nos and another under-age evening pint before we bed down for the night! Next morning it's a long slog to Bwlch summit, where the road is crossed by the Neath to Brecon railway line, and we follow this above the shores of the Crai Reservoir. There is no chance of seeing a train as there's only one a day each way and it's some hours hence (it was closed in 1962).

The attractive Crai Reservoir, which is the main water supply for Swansea, is below the main A4067 road and formerly also the Neath & Brecon railway line, which closes two years after our walk. We see no trains this day as there is only one per day, and this runs in the late afternoon.

After Crai, we turn left onto a minor road to Trecastle, then left again on the A40 Brecon to Llandovery main road. Soon after, we leave this and on to a rough military road over Mynydd Eppynt (and its firing range). A red flag is flying, and a notice warns us not to proceed whilst it is so. After waiting an hour, we hear no guns, so assume it's all clear. Not so as shortly after, an army truck is seen approaching, "What are you f...ing idiots up to? You'll get your heads blown off" is near enough to what I predict will be said, and we are ordered to take a circuitous route to the west. This adds a couple of miles to the walk, and when we arrive at the hamlet of Tirabad, we make camp out of sheer exhaustion.

With no more firing ranges in prospect, we resume northwards next morning through Llanwrtyd Wells, pass under the Central Wales Railway, cross the A483, and up a beautiful valley towards Abergwesyn. We find a remote café run from the front room of a large house and enjoy tea and cakes. Here, our teacher arrives in his car to check on progress and takes a group photo for posterity. Our next objective is the Elan Valley, but it isn't going to be achieved this night. Ahead of us is a formidable mountain, the weather is closing in, and we are tired. We spot a farmhouse with smoke coming from the chimney, so someone must be in. It is occupied by an old man standing in front of a blazing fire in an empty room. He speaks little

English but is friendly and struggles to translate from Welsh. "Well, boyss bach, what brings you here?" We explain as best we can, and he tells us he sold out to the Forestry Commission and comes every evening for old times' sake. He is happy for us to sleep on the floor in our sleeping bags and banks up the fire when he leaves. What a wonderful experience!

The next day we head up the mountain and, at the summit, look down on a beautiful Elan Valley. It's a steep drop into the valley, and we emerge at the Caban Coch reservoir and the first of four impressive dams. Despite being unnatural, it's a delightful walk along this flooded valley. At the north end, we come to a minor east-west road at Pont-ar-Elan, stay on it for a mile, then over a ridge leading to the Wye Valley and our next camp site at Neuadd Ddu. Lying awake in my sleeping bag and hearing traffic pass on the nearby A470, I long to get in a car and be transported to a nice warm bed! The feeling passes, and by morning, I'm raring to go again, even though the rain has set in. We get moving along the A470 to Llangurig, then towards Llanidloes. To our right are the remnants of a railway embankment that goes on for several miles. I later find out this never has any track laid on it and is part of the aborted Manchester and Milford Railway. At Llanidloes, we turn left and take a winding mountain road leading to curiously named Staylittle, at the summit of the road which goes on to Machynlleth. Apparently, it was named as a stopping point for the stagecoaches to rest the horses; not surprising, given the steep road on either approach. We, too, are exhausted and look for somewhere to stay the night. This turns out to be a farm where we are offered a barn and to sleep on the hay. The farmer's wife will cook for us in the morning but only if we all wash thoroughly; it seems a good deal and typifies the friendliness of those we meet.

The beauty of this part-man-made landscape greets our descent from the mountain to the Elan Valley.

Refreshed by a hearty breakfast and unusually clean, we head off into the lush green valley towards Llanbrynmair, where we cross the A483 road and pass under the Cambrian main line (as a steam locomotive crosses over), then on a minor road to the north. The Wynnstay Arms is here, so we stop for our third pint this trip. Upon leaving, we spot an ominous blue light and a police sign, so we make our way in haste! Near Mallwyd, we camp in a farmer's field. The weather has been fair all day, but rain sets in overnight. By morning, it's heavy and persistent, so we decide to dig in for the rest of the day and night. We've no food, so I plod across to the farm, and all they can offer is eggs. I buy two dozen, and we boil them for breakfast, lunch, and supper, passing the time with an all-day card-playing session; and still it rains!

The road out of Llanidloes leads up the valley of the river Clywedog and reaches its summit near Staylittle. Some years later, the valley is flooded, creating the massive and attractive Llyn Clywedog reservoir, with the road diverted in the process. Beyond Staylittle, the road forks, and we drop down steeply to Llanbrynmair. The other branch heads to Machynlleth; it has a lookout point with a compass pointing to distant mountains and is a memorial to writer and broadcaster Wynford Vaughan Thomas, who crossed Wales by many modes, including on horseback in the 1950s.

The next day is a little better as we walk up the steep hill, join the A470 and a long steep climb through Dinas Mawddwy to the summit in the pouring rain. Now we are exhausted and decide to try our luck by splitting up into twos and 'thumbing' a lift. Jeff and I are lucky when a Morris Traveller full of family members and luggage manages to squeeze us two drowned rats into the rear luggage compartment and takes us to Dolgellau. Here, I decide to call it a day when I find I can get a train to Chester, where a friend lives. Jeff decides to get a lift back to Neath whilst I enjoy the luxury of a train ride through Bala and the Vale of Llangollen.

My problems aren't over. Roger is on holiday, and I sleep the night in the Chester station waiting room before being turned out in the early morning by a policeman who is convinced that I'm running away from home when in fact, it's quite the opposite! He tells me to get the first train out, no matter where, so I find myself booking a child return to Liverpool. As I ask for this, the copper points out that I told him I am sixteen, so it's a full fare! When I return to Chester, he's gone, so I ask for a child single to Neath by the cheapest route. Thus, I travel over an amazing route via Oswestry, Welshpool, Newtown, Builth, and Brecon, arriving at Neath Riverside on the only train of the day, at 20:00.

The afternoon train to Chester arriving at Dolgellau.

My Great Welsh Cycle Ride | (Cannock) Welshpool to Neath

I simply can't help myself! Not content with walking to North Wales, three months later, I decide to cycle south through three-quarters of the country. A friend of mine, Trevor, whose parents – both schoolteachers – move from Neath to Cannock in Staffordshire. I make several visits there and on the final one in July 1960, take my bike on the train with the intention of cycling back to Neath with Trevor. It is to be my inaugural experience of Youth Hostels. Cannock is on the A5 Watling Street, another Roman road and rather more famous than Sarn Helen I had walked back at Easter. We take this road, which even back then is busy with traffic, to Shrewsbury, where we have our first hostelling experience. From there, we cycle west, coming into Wales some miles east of Welshpool, taking a secondary road south to Montgomery, where our next hostel is situated. Given that it's the name of one of the Welsh counties, I am quite surprised to find this town is very small and has a much smaller youth hostel than the previous one at Shrewsbury.

From here, we take the back roads to Newtown, passing through the village of Kerry, at one time at the end of a branch railway from Abermule. Re-joining the A483, we pass through Newtown and head west, turning just short of Caersws, onto the southbound A470, crossing over the Cambrian main line, and then following the route of the Moat Lane-Brecon railway to Llanidloes. That evening, we are booked in at Neuadd Ddu hostel, which just happens to be yards away from my campsite on the North Wales walk at Easter. It seems this place is fated as it again rains relentlessly through the night and into the next day, so it's time to don my bright yellow cape and 'sou-wester' hat for the ride to Builth Wells via Rhayader. We stay at another hostel here, and I wander up to the station to see a train from Brecon arrive.

Cyclist in beautiful Mid Wales *(cyclingwales.co.uk)*.

From Builth, our route is on the A470 most of the way to Brecon, a pleasant ride along the River Wye to Llyswen, where we take a hilly road to arrive at Bishop's Meadow, a transport café north of Brecon. We spend some time in Brecon and head west on the A40, then the A4067 at Sennybridge. At Crai, the road from Trecastle comes in from the right, and we retrace southbound my Easter route to Craig-y-Nos. From here, it's back to Neath via Ystradgynlais and the Swansea Valley.

My Great Welsh Car Journey   1965 Neath to Ruabon

It is somewhat surprising that I don't make a car journey further north than Brecon for the first 22 years of my life, and my earliest opportunity to drive to North Wales comes by surprise. I am taking my scout troop to the Welsh Jamboree at Ruabon, near Wrexham. My local scout commissioner has a Ford Anglia but doesn't feel up to a long day's drive, so asks me to do it, which I readily accept. The scouts, meanwhile, go by special train laid on by the Welsh Scout Council.

I have done the route so many times since, and it is very busy and less scenic than other routes, but for the record, our trip is A4067 to Sennybridge, A40 to Brecon, A470 to Builth Wells, and finally, the A483 to Ruabon, and vice-versa. It is a great week's camping, and I fit in a train ride to and from Chester on a day out (it is still a steam train, albeit with an ex-LMS locomotive on an ex-GWR line). Unlike my walking and cycle tours, I recall very few details of the journey except that it is long and tedious. Since those days, I have travelled many thousands of miles to and from North Wales by car in all kinds of weather and know every route and rat-run, and more importantly, where to get food and toilets out of hours!

My Great Welsh Bus Journey — 1999 Swansea to Caernarfon

Even if I wished, I would be hard pressed to find a viable way to travel by bus (to coach standards) all the way to North Wales. Only one service exists, '*Traws Cambria,*' and it has a somewhat chequered history. In the late 1990s, I am engaged by the Wales Tourist Board to produce a directory of bus services in Wales suitable for visitors coming to and getting around the country. Part of this involves product testing, and one of these tests I carry out on this daily service between Cardiff and Caernarfon.

On a fine June day in 1999, I join at Swansea. However, on this day, it is not a coach but a substitute Stagecoach bus. The lower standard of comfort is made up for by a great driver with exemplary customer skills and a good line in banter, and the journey goes faster. It is a very scenic route to Aberystwyth – via Carmarthen, Lampeter, and Aberaeron – where a one-hour, much-needed break is scheduled. To my surprise and relief, is a change of vehicle. From here north, it is a more modern coach operated by the company Arriva. Through tickets are valid, so the change is seamless.

The journey north of Aberystwyth is by the outstandingly scenic route via Machynlleth, Dolgellau, and Porthmadog, terminating in Caernarfon in late afternoon. Despite delays at Porthmadog, we arrive on time. In the evening, out of curiosity, I take a bus to Dinas Dinlle and Caernarfon airport, which is being actively considered for an air link from Cardiff. I laugh out loud…. they can't be serious!

The changeover of buses is routinely made at Aberystwyth (seen here in 2003), conveniently at lunchtimes. Stagecoach operates the southern leg and Arriva the northern. In recent years an expanded network of long-distance bus routes has developed in Wales with connections at key points (Chapter 4).

My Great Welsh Air Journey | 2007 Cardiff to Valley (Anglesey)

After the establishment of the Welsh Assembly in 1999, I suppose it was possible that a project that had been aired – and rejected – several times would be reconsidered in the emerging grand plans to link North and South Wales faster. Through train services are introduced, but still, it takes around four hours. Apart from a lack of demand, the availability of suitable airports in the north is a major stumbling block. The use of Hawarden in the northeast seems feasible until realised as incompatible with the airport's military and testing roles for British Aerospace. Dinas near Caernarfon is briefly considered and rejected on the grounds of poor conditions and remoteness. This view is reinforced by my 1999 visit. Finally, Valley, a military facility near Holyhead, is chosen, and various problems are ironed out to permit a twice-daily service from Cardiff.

So it is that on 10th October 2007, I join the evening flight from Cardiff for the one-hour journey to Valley. I am part of a small group from *CILT Cymru Wales* (a professional transport institution), and the journey purpose is for a national committee meeting in Llandudno the following day. The aircraft in the early days is a Jetstream 21, the junior equivalent of the *Jetstream 41* on erstwhile Cardiff-Paris flights, operated by *Air Wales*. Despite its grand name, it is a turboprop and has a modest 19 seats, of which 17 are taken on this trip. There is not a lot to say about this, as half the journey is in darkness and only takes an hour. The problems of Valley's remoteness are solved by chartering a minibus to get us to Llandudno. We all enjoy the journey and return by train the next day.

Looking back, I don't think I realise that I am probably one of the only people to have crossed Wales south to north on foot, by bike, car, train, bus, and now, by plane!!

I use the service again in 2016, now operated by *Links Air*, and it's a 17-seater. The morning flight from Cardiff is again a one-way journey for me, leaving at 07:40 with just six on board, including me. Disappointingly, it is cloudy leaving Cardiff but then over Aberystwyth, the cloud clears, and I enjoy the most amazing and beautiful view of the Cambrian Coast I've ever seen, and it only cost me £29.50 one-way! However, the five-mile taxi journey to Holyhead costs me a further £20! The worst deal is that for the Welsh taxpayer, who has subsidised my journey by over £100, but, hey-ho, who cares when it's such a super trip!

The small and stylish aeroplane used by Links Air in 2016 is seen leaving Valley airport on its return flight to Cardiff. It has arrived with 6 passengers and returns with just 3 on board, hardly economic!

In June 2022, after more than two years of suspension due to the pandemic, the Welsh Government finally pulls the plug and advises people to use the train.

An interesting and expensive experiment!

Crewe, the centre of the British railway universe

My travels of the past 70+ years have taken me to all corners (and many high points) of the United Kingdom and the Republic of Ireland, and I've clocked up almost a million and a half miles, about two-thirds of this on surface public transport. It is impractical for me to cover travel to all parts of these islands in any detail, so I have necessarily been selective, choosing those journeys or areas that interest me or are, I believe, of special interest to travel enthusiasts.

That potentially leaves a lot of journeys, places, incidents, and anecdotes that I believe are best included in this compendium of experiences which cover a wide range of topics and things of general interest. These are sub-divided into several themes. The first relates mainly to my experiences in the largely steam-operated world of railways up to the watershed of 1968, the official end of steam in the UK. There are some anecdotes relating to other transport and finally, some of the wonderful places and sights in these isles.

Cruising the Bristol Channel has been popular for years in the 'M.V. Balmoral

When steam is king and I am impressionable

43 years later, 70000 'Britannia' on a special train at Neath

In the winter of 1952/53, my father springs a surprise by taking me to Neath station to see an early evening arrival from Paddington. It is dark, and through the gloom, as I hear an unfamiliar chime whistle, a strange beast appears, bearing the exciting name 'Shooting Star.' It's the initial trip by the newly built Britannia-class locomotives, which take over from the 'Castles' on Paddington to Swansea trains, and I'm thrilled to see the first one! Similar looking to a 'Britannia' with distinctive differences is the famous 'Evening Star,' the last steam locomotive to be built for British Railways in 1960. In September 1964, my friends and I are invited to help steward a children's excursion from Swansea to Swindon sponsored by Lyons Maid ice cream. In exchange, we get a free trip, and I get a further bonus of a footplate ride between Cardiff and Swansea on the return journey!

Weekly Runabout tickets are a must-have as they allow unlimited cheap travel in an area for a week. On our holiday in Eastbourne in 1956, I use mine each morning to go to Brighton and back before breakfast just to see the 08:00 departure to Plymouth, always a 'Bulleid Pacific' steam locomotive, a different one every day. The ticket is also valid on the Sussex branch lines based on Tunbridge Wells, a fascinating rural network entirely operated by steam power. Alas, it is unremunerative and largely gone by 1970 save for stub branches to East Grinstead and Uckfield.

Prior to joining British Rail in 1961, I arrange a trip on a freight train in northeast England. It is one carrying iron ore between Tyne Dock in South Shields and Consett steelworks. I arrive at the dock office early, show my permit, and the controller checks if the ore trains will be running that day. Fortunately, a ship has docked, and there are several, each carrying over 500 tonnes of iron ore in special automatic tipping wagons and, due to steep grades, needing a large steam locomotive at front and rear on the steepest sections. The guard, it turns out, is from Neath, and I enjoy an exciting and very educational trip.

This photograph *(by Ben Brooksbank)* shows the *first* Severn Bridge, which carries the Severn & Wye Railway between Lydney and Sharpness. On Sunday, 23 October 1960, I'm on a diverted Cardiff to Birmingham train over the bridge due to work on the line between Lydney and Gloucester. The diversion is a pleasant surprise as the line is on my 'to do' list. Two days later, Tuesday night, 25 October, it is reported on the news that the bridge has been struck by two barges, and the centre span has collapsed. The bridge is never rebuilt.

A very significant train in October 1965 heralds the reopening of one of the first standard-gauge heritage lines in the country, the 'Dart Valley.' On this trip, seen at Parson's Tunnel, Dawlish, privately-owned ex-GWR tank 4555, and tender locomotive 3205 take a special train from Exeter to Totnes, where both are to go into storage at Buckfastleigh, though it isn't

4555 and 3205 double head a special train to Buckfastleigh along the attractive coastal route at Dawlish

until April 1969 that operations commence on the Dart Valley. 4555 transfers to nearby Dartmouth Steam Railway on its opening in 1973, and 3205 remains at Buckfastleigh.

The railway in Bradford in early 1967 has that run-down feel, and despite changes in subsequent years, it persists to some extent. In that year, there are remnants of steam operation daily; trains to London King's Cross run from Exchange station as portions of the main Leeds train, to be attached at Wakefield Westgate. From Forster Square station, similar short trains attach to the main train for London St Pancras at Leeds City. All are operated by a small fleet of run-down ex-LMS tank locomotives. The most interesting weekday train is the 08:20 Halifax to King's Cross, with just 3 coaches, via Huddersfield (reverse) and Wakefield Kirkgate (reverse) to Wakefield Westgate, where its coaches are shunted on the rear of the main train. On arrival at Wakefield Westgate, it attaches to the rear of the London train. On one summer Saturday, I take a holiday train from Bradford to Bridlington on its fascinating route through West Yorkshire. It is hauled by a Standard Class 5 and travels via Halifax, Elland, Horbury, Wakefield, Castleford, Goole, and the avoiding line at Hull. Other interesting trains, steam-hauled from West Yorkshire on Saturdays, run from Leeds to Llandudno and to Blackpool. Another runs from Leeds to Bournemouth via Huddersfield, Penistone, Sheffield Victoria, and the former 'Great Central' route as far as Banbury, then on the direct route avoiding Reading. By 1966, it has shed its steam power and is usually hauled by an EE type 3 diesel.

In the gloomy and dirty surroundings of Bradford Exchange station, a Fairburn tank locomotive awaits its departure to Wakefield on a London train.

It is summer 1966 and swan song of steam on the Cambrian lines with most Saturday extras steam hauled. Robert and I arrive at Machynlleth to see the Pwllheli portion of the Birmingham train, and there is an error; it should have coupled to the Aberystwyth portion at Dovey Junction. Then the westbound train arrives double-headed, with a portion for Aberystwyth and Pwllheli. The inside locomotive is low on coal and must go on to shed.

High noon, a 'train jam' at Machynlleth

Meanwhile, the eastbound train is shunted to allow the Aberystwyth train to arrive, and its locomotive is also low on coal and must also go on to shed. The ensuing mêlée is too difficult to explain in a few words; suffice to say, we witness an almighty 'train jam' that takes well over an hour to sort out!!

At a time of much decline in railway traffic, there are occasional glimmers of hope that things will get better. One such is the launch of the new West Coast Main Line electric service in April 1966 when I and two railway colleagues in the Cardiff office decide to be there on the opening day, travelling up to London and then taking an all-electric service from Euston to Manchester Piccadilly and back. We are most impressed and hope this is a sign of things to come. Our locomotive is E3136 both ways, seen here at London Euston.

A Maritime interlude

Ferries, an 'Air Line' and a sailing ship

Ferry across the Mersey, Birkenhead in the background

The maritime city of Liverpool and I have many and varied liaisons, which I regard as a love-hate relationship. My first introduction is in 1960 (chapter 3) as I arrive around 06:30 in the morning tired, hungry, and short of money, having been forced out of temporary lodgings at the Chester station waiting room on the first train by an unsympathetic policeman. Liverpool isn't at its best, and I get out quickly.

The 1970s sees three visits, first in late 1972 when I arrive with a party of scouts from Neath. I am to take them to a first division football match, and we travel there cheaply on a 'mystery' excursion. I am informed the secret destination has two football clubs with different names, so it must be Liverpool, and we watch Everton v West Ham.

I go twice for job interviews; in 1974 and 1978, and in neither am I successful. In the second, I am there for a passenger sales position under the legendary and late Ron Cotton, who goes on to become the saviour of the Settle & Carlisle line. I get notice to attend as I return from my first USA trip badly jet-lagged, and by the time of the interview, my body clock is at midnight, and I have difficulty keeping awake. I am destined not to work in Liverpool!

As British Rail Manager for Wales, I have a route under my stewardship that goes into Merseyside (Wrexham-Bidston), and I court controversy when I advertise the service as Wrexham to Liverpool (via Bidston). Sometime in the late 80s/early 90s, I am railroaded into taking the chair of a group representing Chester and North Wales to lobby for direct links to the Channel Tunnel. I think it's a 'dead duck,' but the group prevails on me to give a positive spin at a conference at the Adelphi Hotel in Liverpool. I travel with a Welsh Office representative, and we go on the legendary Mersey Ferry the evening before; it's such a slick operation that we notice an evidently drunk passenger who can't get off in time either in Birkenhead or in Liverpool, so he must have spent all evening going back and forth! Next day at the conference, I give a rousing presentation, not believing a word of what I'm saying, and get a large round of applause for my trouble!

Another business trip in 1978 takes me to Hull, where I am to make arrangements for the rapid transport of high-quality steel from Port Talbot works to a heating appliance customer in the city. I am free to go whichever way I please within reason, so I take the train via Doncaster and

P.S. Farringford leaving Hull Corporation Pier

Immingham, then the local to New Holland for the paddle steamer 'Lincoln Castle,' soon to be withdrawn when the Humber Bridge opens. I stay the night, go to a small private cinema. Its ten or so customers are addressed by a tearful manager who announces it is his last night!

Not maritime except it is a crossing of a river, Emirates Air Line is a visitor attraction more than public transport. In London, with my wife attending a conference in Euston Road, I take time out to travel over the fascinating Docklands Light Railway, which I liken to a giant 'Hornby' train set. The Air Line is a bonus (as it's there), and I take a one-way trip to Greenwich. Not so the family in my pod on a return journey; kids tease mother about dropping in the river, and father says water contact is **not** a soft landing!

The car ferries between Fishguard and Rosslare have been plying for over 50 years. The 'M.V. Felicity' has been the regular ferry and is occasionally replaced when needing a refit. Having arrived at Rosslare in June 1997, we are

surprised to see its replacement, the 'M.V. Koningen Beatrix' in the harbour for a changeover, the latter a veteran of the Harwich-Hook of Holland route.

Pleasure steamers ply the Bristol Channel for many years, dwindling to just two vessels by the 1980s. There is a most interesting excursion in June 1970 as Hugh has booked a day out on the 'M.V. Balmoral' from Mumbles Pier to Lundy, a fascinating trip in glorious weather. The ship cannot dock at the quayside, so it is met by a small 'tender' to get us to land. This small island is a fascinating place with a fine pub, the Marisco Tavern, serving its home-brewed beer from the cask.

Moving on to South Devon, I enjoy an interesting day trip in June 1976. An excursion train is run from Swansea to Totnes with a trip down the River Dart to Dartmouth. As we approach the latter, I spot two very interesting sights: in the foreground, the famous 'Charlotte Rhodes' clipper used in filming the 'Onedin Line,' and behind, the return excursion awaiting our arrival at Kingswear with a double-headed 'Lydham

Manor' and world-famous 'Flying Scotsman' which are to take us back to Paignton before a class 47 diesel back to Swansea. A pretty good value day out!

A land of infinite variety

Over many years of travel, it would have been surprising if I had not come across lots of fascinating things about the history, landscape, and seasons, so I have selected some of those that interest me.

This could just as well have been a painting by the famous artist John Constable whose stamping ground was mainly in Essex and Suffolk. Here, in Shropshire at the Ironbridge Gorge Museum. I have organised an outing for the Neath Camera Club, whose members find plenty of things to work on and produce some amazing photographs. This must be my personal best showing a coal barge on the restored local industrial canal. A great day out except for our coach driver, who vows never to come here again! after having to negotiate its precipitous grades!

When I go to work in East Anglia, I am surprised to find how few windmills there are (once dominating whole landscapes). Those remaining are mostly restored as dwellings or small business premises and retained in situ with regular maintenance. They look wonderful in any setting but particularly

in spectacular lighting, such as this one in Cley next the Sea on the coast of North Norfolk.

Also in East Anglia, here is a picture of a once common sight at the seaside, a 'Punch & Judy' show for children. In 1980, I discover one still very much in play in the attractive seaside

town of Southwold. This is, in my view, one of the nicest such towns in England with the bonus of hosting one of England's most famous real ale breweries, Adnams. At the time, real ale is almost extinct in East Anglia, so this must be a haven for us aficionados of good beer. The pubs around here specialise in game pies, and I also get an introduction to samphire, a sea marsh delicacy, much better than the imported stuff we get nowadays.

Back to industrial archaeology, during my time working in Leeds, I get to like the rugged mill towns though

many of their woollen mills are being phased out, become derelict, or turned into mail order warehouses. Years later, I take a two-day drive around the north of England, looking at these industrial remains. Most of the time, the light is not conducive to good photography but improves when I arrive at Halifax, surely one of the best-preserved mill towns in Yorkshire. I love the name 'slubbing dyers!'

I'm not sure whether this is a clever bit of open-air artwork or a very orderly deck chair

attendants' work, but these chairs – laid out in a partly organised, partly random way – are not occupied by anybody, but that may just be down to the dull weather that day. The scene is at the small south Devon resort of Beer, close to Seaton. It's a lovely little town though I'm disappointed not to find any decent beer there; maybe its name is derived from something else!

I am fortunate to join a two-day visit to Northumbria laid on by its Tourist Board in the early 1980s, which is hoping British Rail will run day excursions there. Accordingly, I discover a part of England that is virtually unknown to me and many others in the group as we are shown Hadrian's Wall, Alnwick Castle,

Beamish Museum, and Craster Kipper Smokery. To cap it all is Bamburgh Castle on its most commanding site above the North Sea. I get a surprise here finding the epic film 'El Cid' was partly shot here with the massed armies on the extensive beach.

The attractive harbour at Aberaeron, the gem of the Ceredigion coast with its colourful buildings.

The Most Beautiful Country in the World

I can say this with confidence as one who has made countless journeys through Wales since the early '50s, travelled very extensively in Europe and North America (From Hell to Paradise and a thousand places in between) and I'm probably in the top thousand people for total miles travelled around the country.

There are few areas of Wales where I haven't been, yet it is still possible to discover places that I didn't know existed, such as in 2012 when I find myself at Loggerheads (place not mindset) Country Park in north-east Wales on a tourism thematic group visit. At that time, I stay with Josiane at a country hotel in Llandrillo, which is among the top places to eat in Britain.

It is not possible in a chapter to cover everything I love about Wales, so I will confine myself to a selection of areas, places, and journeys that appeal most to me:

- The Gower Peninsula and the Gower Coast Path
- The Pembrokeshire and Ceredigion Coasts
- The Brecon Beacons National Park
- Snowdonia and the Cambrian Coast and Mountains
- Magical bus journeys around Wales

All will include comments and anecdotes on the transport scene.

The Gower Peninsula...   **... and its scenic Coast Path**

Fall Bay, Gower is less than a mile from Rhossili, but it feels like it's a million miles from anywhere!

Gower, Britain's first *Area of Outstanding Natural Beauty* (*AONB*) in 1956, is virtually unknown to me in the early years of my life, despite its boundary being a mere 15 miles from home. Prior to 1969, the only visits are on family day trips to Langland and Caswell Bays and one trip deeper into Gower, to Oxwich Bay. I think it is in summer 1952 that the family has an outing there in the *Wolseley 14*, a brute of a car, though not robust enough to avoid disaster on the steep Oxwich hill. Even in those days, there is traffic congestion, and I recall it climbing in fits and starts until the engine boils and a nasty brown liquid comes from the bonnet! Dad stops and searches for something to pour water into the radiator and cool it enough to continue. Another day, in Langland Bay, we are on the beach when the heavens open, and there's a mass exodus to the bus stop. A fleet of single-deck buses with two rear axles – necessary for the steep hill – arrive in no time, and everybody is moved swiftly to nearby Oystermouth bus station to connect with the 'Mumbles Train' to Swansea (coordination between modes at its best).

From 1969, I spend many winter weekends at the youth hostel at Port Eynon, and this continues for several years. I learn how beautiful Gower is, and it whets my appetite for more. Years later, there is an interesting experience when an exhibition comes to Swansea to draw attention to the plight of *Native American* tribes, and my stepdaughter Nathalie is asked by their leader, Gerald – a descendant of 'Crazy Horse' – if we can take him to see Gower. It's a most interesting day, and over coffee, in Rhossili, he talks of common misconceptions; the real name for 'Sioux' is 'Lakota'; the 'Battle of Wounded Knee' is a 'Massacre,' and as he marvels at the number of trees in Gower, we discover that there are virtually no trees in his native South Dakota!

Outings to the peninsula are occasional then in the present century, a very interesting opportunity arises with the introduction of an innovative bus network on Gower. I approach Swansea Council in the hope they will engage me and my colleague, Colin Speakman, to develop and implement a marketing plan. We are successful and prepare a strategy for 'Gower Explorer' generating huge growth. A spin-off is a supporting partnership, 'BayTrans,' which continues to this day promoting leisure travel by sustainable means.

Rhossili and Worm's Head.

I become firmly established in Gower and Swansea Bay in general and now actively promote travel in the wonderful land- and seascapes and along the invigorating walks on the Gower Coast Path. It helps greatly to "walk the walk" so to speak, and I'm proud to have completed the circumnavigation of the Peninsula in eight stages, a distance of over 50 miles. The coastlines of Gower can rightly be described as very spectacular, and I look back with pride on sixteen years of promoting sustainable travel and meeting interesting people. Visitors – from all over the world – make up 20-30% of summer bus travellers! A highlight is walking the Coast Path and its promotion through the web and social media, with the luxury of choosing to go when the weather is good, creating an accurate text and photographic record. The buses are well run with a good local operator supported by Council funds, and to this day, the level of service remains the same despite several changes of operators. Below is a selection of stunning images of Gower.

Three Cliffs Bay

From the Gower Coast Path at Nicholaston

The Stunning Pembrokeshire and Ceredigion coasts

The harbour at Tenby is one of the most attractive features of this lovely coastal resort.

I am introduced to Pembrokeshire from an early age, spending a family holiday in Tenby in 1948 (all that I remember then is going to see the 'Sunderland Flying Boats' in Pembroke Dock). In the 1950s, I attend two scout camps, one in Saundersfoot and the other in Broad Haven. At the former, I live up to my reputation as an inveterate explorer by walking the coast trail solo – a former mineral railway with two tunnels extant – to Wiseman's Bridge near Kilgetty. We use the train to get to the camps, and I recall our 1955 journey to Saundersfoot is heavily delayed as the train is too long for the passing loop at Narberth with much shunting and faffing around! Further camping trips are made in the late 60s and early 70s, usually to St Brides, and in these years, I really get to love this part of Wales. Walks on the 'Pembrokeshire Coast Path', visits to secluded beaches and coves, and mackerel freshly cooked on the Little Haven sea wall are all part of the magic lure of this county.

In the early 1970s, my sales role with the railway takes me again to southwest Wales. Most of my clients are small businesses ranging from fresh flowers and milk for London markets to corgi dog breeders. All, alas, long since gone from the railways and much diminished in general.

The magnificent view over St Brides Bay, Pembrokeshire, from our camp site

I also have an after-sales role with the three major oil refineries despatching by rail and am not a little surprised as to how well they blend into the coastal landscape. In the mid 80's/ early 90s, I return as marketing and development manager for passenger train services in South and West Wales. I naturally travel extensively by train and appreciate the value of the railway to this deeply rural and beautiful tourism area. I return to camping in southwest Wales again this time, often to St Brides Bay and to Dinas Cross near Fishguard. I take a liking for north Pembrokeshire, which is wilder and more rugged than the more popular south.

Industry co-exists with a beautiful natural landscape, Dale

Following early retirement, I move into other fields, including consultancy, which occasionally involves working in west Wales, but with more time to spend on day visits and short holidays purely for leisure. Josiane and I share a liking for the area and have several firm favourites – St David's, Lamphey, Penally, and Tenby – for short breaks. We take to the fine Ceredigion coastline, and another favourite is the sumptuous and colourful town of Aberaeron.

During the dark days of the pandemic, we make several day trips to Laugharne (of Dylan Thomas, the poet, fame), Saundersfoot, Tenby, and Aberaeron.

I am also able to reflect on times past and note with pleasure the expansion of passenger train service with more modern rolling stock and quality uplift (masking some diminution of service levels) of local bus services, including the innovative 'Puffin Shuttle' coastal bus routes for walkers. A network of 'Traws Cymru' long-distance buses grows serving Carmarthen, Haverfordwest, Fishguard, and Aberaeron.

Newgale in St Brides Bay, North Pembrokeshire

It is notable that there are areas – where train services are withdrawn in the 1960s – that are still poorly served by public transport, particularly the rural area between Whitland and Cardigan, and I travel on the final day of service in 1962. It is a wonderful, meandering line (known as the 'Cardi Bach') serving nowhere much except Cardigan, and a journey from Carmarthen can take up to three hours compared to an hour by road!

Glorious days of steam: a summer Saturday holiday express arrives Tenby in July 1963

In contrast, the route to Fishguard Harbour, a major force in the local economy until the early 60s with several freight trains, boat trains, and even a local service to Clarbeston Road, has a declining influence as a rail/sea route to Ireland. It is rejuvenated with extra trains and a reopened and well-appointed station at Goodwick in 2012.

Despite the effects of the pandemic, I've managed to make several journeys on the Pembroke and Milford routes, which are now well served by fully refurbished trains in the smart new Transport for Wales livery. Towards the end of 2022, there will be a complete metamorphosis of rolling stock with brand new trains, which are expected to transform travel further.

Left: A very successful Pembrokeshire transport initiative are the Coastal Shuttles designed for walkers. Here the 'Puffin Shuttle' is at the beautiful coastal village of Little Haven.
Right: Another successful transport initiative is the re-opening of Fishguard and Goodwick train station.

The Brecon Beacons National Park...   **... and Waterfall Country**

A spectacular early evening view of the twin Beacons peaks, Pen-y-fan (near right) and Corn Du (far right).

This is the closest national park to my home and one which I know well over much of my life. My first contact is quite an extensive, if short-lived one, as I take train trips from Neath to Brecon and use connections thereon to Newport, Hereford, and Moat Lane Junction, all of which pass through the national park over sections of their routes. However, it is all too fleeting as the trains from Neath cease in October 1962, followed by the other Brecon routes just two months later. Since then, there has been no station in the park, although Abergavenny, Llandovery, Llandeilo, and Merthyr Tydfil all lie on the boundary. In chapter 8, you can read more about the Brecon to Moat Lane Junction line.

From 1963, all my journeys in the area are by road, mainly by car, and occasionally by bus. The area of the national park ranges from wild mountains to lush pastoral scenery and has within its boundaries the highest mountains in South Wales, 'Pen-y-Fan' (2906 feet) and 'Corn Du' (2864 feet), though neither quite make the status of a 'Munro' (>3000 feet). My ascents of these and other mountains can be found in Chapter 7. As well as the lovely countryside, the national park has several fascinating towns, the most prominent being Brecon, the most popular, World Class 'Book Town' Hay-on-Wye, has an annual literary festival which I attend often.

A Brecon train at Neath Riverside station in summer 1962.

60 years on, it's the T6 Traws Cymru bus to Brecon *(Stephen Miles)*

In 2010, one of my most successful consultancy projects is when I am engaged by the national park authority to plan a festival bus link between the railhead at Hereford and Hay-on-Wye. Prior to this, those arriving by public transport are very few as the main link is an expensive taxi journey. The service quickly expands, and passenger numbers grow from about 1000 users in year one to well over 5000 within a few years, needing double-deckers to take the loads.

Most main roads in the national park converge on Brecon, and they enjoy a frequent bus service, part of the 'Traws Cymru' network. These generally run seven days a week and in all weathers. All the routes are highly scenic and are gradually building up a good tourist clientele. There is just one railway remaining in the National Park boundaries, the narrow-gauge Brecon Mountain Railway tourist operation from Pant near Merthyr Tydfil to remote Torpantau, the former summit of the standard-gauge Newport to Brecon railway line, which closes in 1962. I have the unique pleasure of travelling on both original and tourist trains!

Waterfall Country

I will now take you to a part of the national park known locally as 'Waterfall Country,' which has the finest collection of spectacular waterfalls in the British Isles. Consisting of the two main and several secondary tributaries of the river Neath and a tributary of the river Tawe. They are a big challenge for walkers as they pass through limestone country containing several well-known caves. It's notable that the largest cave system in Western Europe can be found in the Swansea Valley, known as 'Dan-yr-Ogof, National Showcaves of Wales'; there is a significant complex at 'Porth-yr-Ogof' near Ystradfellte.

The most spectacular waterfall is on the river Hepste easternmost tributary of the river Neath. 'Scŵd-yr-Eira' is a waterfall, and it is possible to walk behind it; the falling water as the river tips over a shelf of hard rock which erodes and collapses over millennia.

The two main tributaries, the Nedd Fechan and the Mellte, are separated by upland of outstanding natural beauty, especially as seen on a cold winter day.

Snowdonia	Cambrian Mountains and Coast

The magnificent view looking up the Mawddach estuary from Barmouth.

There aren't enough superlatives to describe the sheer beauty of this part of Mid and North Wales. The poet Shelley is alleged to have quoted, "There is only one view more beautiful than that looking up the Mawddach Estuary, and that is the view looking down the Mawddach Estuary." He was, of course, there long before the railway and Barmouth viaduct was to make the view even more spectacular. In chapter 8, I will be covering the Cambrian Coast railway journey in more detail. Here I will describe my travels and impressions of this area, mostly by car, though I frequently travel on the Conwy Valley and Cambrian Coast lines and, prior to its closure in 1965, the beautiful Ruabon to Barmouth route. Earlier this century, I use 'Traws Cymru' bus routes which are on this as well as other routes not served by the railways; and described later in this chapter.

The Cambrian Mountains cover a large area to the south of Snowdonia, and one spectacular journey I often make is that between Llanidloes and Machynlleth, a one-time stagecoach route long devoid of public transport. This passes near the highest mountain in the range, *Plynlimon*, one I climb in 1969, seeking the source of the river Severn which I find in the middle of a bog; however, I'm unimpressed by this mountain. Further north, the scenery gets more rugged, particularly on the A470 road north of Cemmaes Road and the foothills of Cader Idris en route to Dolgellau. This interesting town is built of local grey stone and the crossroads for east-west and north-south routes and a major interchange for 'Traws Cymru' buses.

The Mawddach Estuary east of Dolgellau marks a transition to the Snowdonia area in the north, and from here, the road is spectacular, the Rhinog Mountains separating it from the coastal strip. A bizarre sight at Trawsfynydd is the redundant nuclear power station, destined to be mothballed for a very long time hence. Set against its artificial lake and a wonderful mountain backdrop, it exudes a strange beauty. It is a modern industrial feature though a little further on are the remnants of a once massive slate industry – centred on Blaenau Ffestiniog – with the unenviable reputation as one of the wettest places in Wales. The tips have in many cases, been adapted for modern tourism, but after a rain shower, they can look quite attractive in the sun!

Harlech Castle *(right foreground)* backed by the mountains of Snowdonia

Taking the coast route north can be a very different experience, whether on rail or road. Inland at Tywyn, one can catch sight of the once coastal 'Bird Rock' now miles inland and still hosting cormorants! The massive hulk of 'Cader Idris' stands sentinel over Barmouth and the Mawddach Estuary. North of here, one must look inland to see the other side of the impenetrable barrier between the sea and the interior. The coast has several inlets spanned by the railway – Barmouth and Llandecwyn – but crossed by road only at the latter and that only recently brought up to a high standard as a new road/rail bridge, Pont Brewit. Just to the south is Harlech Castle, the most formidable in Wales and seen to very good effect from the train. The distant mountains of Snowdonia come ever closer, and on a fine day, it's possible to see the summit of Snowdon itself.

The classic view of Snowdon from Capel Curig.

This takes us nicely into the Snowdonia range, of which Snowdon is central and prominent. As well as a limited network of roads through the mountain passes, the area is blessed with two fine narrow-gauge railways radiating from Porthmadog, the original 'Ffestiniog Railway' to Blaenau Ffestiniog and the recently restored spectacular 'Welsh Highland Railway' to Caernarfon. Travel on both routes is a feast for the eyes in dramatic mountain scenery and in the former industrial villages of Beddgelert, Capel Curig, and Llanberis. Now it is the playground of those seeking their thrills in mountaineering or, more recently, in high adrenalin zip wires and the like. The whole area has been served for many years by the 'Snowdon Sherpa' bus with its very picturesque routings between Caernarfon, Betws-y-Coed, Bangor, and Porthmadog. As well as sport, the area has many other attractions, from 'Llechwedd Slate Caverns' at Blaenau Ffestiniog to the well-known 'Swallow Falls' at Betws-y-Coed and narrow-gauge railways centred on Llanberis which include the iconic 'Snowdon Mountain Railway.' Llanberis can be said to be the spiritual centre for mountaineering, and one of its shrines is the 'Pen-y-Gwryd Inn' near Capel Curig, where the 'Everest' conquest of 1953 was conceived. It is an incredible area with which I become familiar mainly through work when I am managing train services for British Rail and later the 'Conwy Valley Community Rail Partnership' for a couple of years. The area leaves an indelible impression.

Connection between the scenic Conwy Valley line and narrow-gauge Ffestiniog Railway at Blaenau Ffestiniog.

Traws Cymru

Magical Bus Journeys Through Wales

Brecon Bus Interchange is one of the principal hubs of the Traws Cymru network.

From the mid-1980s on, I become almost a 'commuter' on the rural roads through Mid Wales and often wonder what treasures a long-distance bus network would open to visitors to our beautiful country. I know the routes well from regular use but, often when driving, fail to see the detail and panorama of landscapes.

There are several long-distance routes in Wales, which are random and uncoordinated. Most complete is the X94 Wrexham to Barmouth via Dolgellau, a remnant of the rail replacement service put in on closure of the parallel railway route. The Cardiff-Caernarfon via Aberystwyth once-daily service (Chapter 3), not strictly a through route, has Aberystwyth connections, and through ticket availability guaranteed. It is an act of faith in the late 1990s when north-south and east-west services connect at Dolgellau and, from the advent of the 'Welsh Assembly' in 1999, steps are taken to create a national network that today is virtually complete. I travel a substantial part of the network in 2005 carrying out independent research on the X32 Caernarfon to Aberystwyth, X94 Barmouth-Wrexham, and 550 Cardigan-Aberystwyth routes:

later, the X40 Carmarthen-Aberystwyth, the T4 Brecon-Cardiff, and T6 Swansea-Brecon. A common thread is the amazing variety of country, mountain, and coastal views.

I inevitably have favourites; the two that interchange at Dolgellau top the list; both thread Snowdonia National Park's spectacular mountain and lakes scenery, the X94 (now T10) passing through iconic towns of Llangollen, Corwen, Bala, and Dolgellau. This route closely mirrors the wonderful railway which was replaced in 1965, particularly the beautiful Vale of Llangollen and Llyn Tegid (Bala Lake).

A feature of the majority of Traws Cymru bus routes is the quite amazing views to be had as the bus negotiates the mountains, valleys, and coasts of rural Wales. One of the finest is the A470/A487 between Dolgellau and Machynlleth, as exemplified by this forward view from the X32 as it negotiates the steep drop towards Talyllyn Lake on its southbound journey in June 2006.

The outstanding scenery of the Vale of Llangollen is seen to great advantage from the T10 bus.

The X32 (now T2) heads from Caernarfon to the coast at Porthmadog, thence back inland on a highly scenic itinerary through Maentwrog and Trawsfynydd to meet the T10 at Dolgellau; then south skirting Cader Idris and taking the mountain pass through Corris to Machynlleth. It crosses the Cambrian railway here and heads south to Aberystwyth via an inland route as the railway is largely a coastal route. Dolgellau is the main hub of various bus routes and retains that busy look with interchange every couple of hours or so.

Those routes through the central 'spine' of Wales, on the A470, A483, and A438, are interesting with completely new itineraries created from a historic single Cardiff-Liverpool service and Brecon-Hereford and Brecon-Merthyr outliers. Built up virtually from nothing, the T4 from Cardiff to Newtown traverses the Brecon Beacons National Park and the important Powys towns of Builth and Llandrindod Wells. It is very spectacular south of Brecon, clinging to the side of South Wales's highest mountain, 'Pen-y-Fan,' at Storey Arms. From Brecon, it follows the route of the Brecon to Moat Lane rail line (Chapter 8) along the highly scenic Wye Valley. Recently, a new service has been added (T14) from Cardiff to Hereford via Brecon and Hay on Wye, a truly bucolic route through Powys and Herefordshire. Finally, the T6 completes the network providing a Swansea connection at Brecon.

The predecessor to the T5 leaves Aberaeron in July 2006 with spectacular Cardigan Bay in the background.

Wild and beautiful Connemara to the west of Galway.

Ireland is as delightful a country as one could wish for, with great scenery, lovely people, and a degree of quirkiness in everyday life. Over many years its railways retain an old-fashioned charm despite steam operation ceasing long before it does on mainland Britain.

Much of the countryside is relatively flat, particularly in the Irish midlands, and this comes as a surprise to me and probably many visitors who are used to images of Ireland's famous coastlines. However, along the east and, more particularly, west and north coasts, substantial areas of the mountain are to be found. I find the most scenic train journeys are Wexford to Bray on the east coast, Athlone to Galway and Westport and Mallow to Tralee on the west, and between Coleraine and Derry in Northern Ireland.

Using a combination of modes, I seek over the years to get to nether regions of the island of Ireland where I take in the most remarkable scenery and, particularly in my early years, a completely different way of life, almost a time-warp in some instances. My narrative includes travels to Counties Donegal and Mayo in the northwest and the Dingle Peninsula and Ring of Kerry in the southwest. I include anecdotes of train journeys in various parts of the country, which epitomise the unconventional nature of this island.

Travelling by Train in Ireland

The railway network in the Irish Republic remains remarkably constant between 1966 and 2000 with the loss of Waterford-Mallow and gain of Limerick-Ennis, and no changes in the North. Irish Railways is entirely diesel locomotive operated (except Dublin commuter) in this period; this picture at Claremorris looks typical of much of the rail system at the time.

I visit the Republic of Ireland numerous times between 1966 and 2000 (and the North several times in the same period) with both countries visited in some years. Most of my travel is by train (6700 miles) though significant car journeys have been made in more recent years. Travel to and from Ireland is usually by sea, by five routes (Fishguard-Rosslare; Swansea-Cork; Holyhead-Dun Laoghaire; Heysham-Belfast, and Stranraer-Larne). I fly in connection with consultancy work in the North and for some other trips.

Trains in the Republic outside Dublin are 100% locomotive operated on timetables that change little over the 34 years. Northern Ireland, by contrast, is almost entirely diesel multiple units operated with a small amount of steam (Belfast-Larne) on my first visit in 1967. If I were to go today, I would see some dramatic changes with most of the Republic's trains and all in the North operated by diesel multiple-units. The Dublin-Belfast Enterprise and Dublin-Cork Intercity lines remain as locomotive-hauled outposts, and a majority of Dublin suburban services are electrically operated on the DART network, and this figure is rapidly expanding.

An Irish Rail Miscellany

Ireland is a small country with a fascinating railway network where amazing and amusing things happen routinely. Here is a chronological digest of some of my experiences:

1966 Rosslare to Dungarvan, County Waterford

My first trip by train in Ireland is in July 1966, taking scouts to summer camp in Stradbally, Co. Waterford. It's a great introduction to a railway that's 100% diesel operated. The train is comfortable with a dining car serving tray meals. It is through from Rosslare to Cork via the long-closed route through Dungarvan.

We alight at the small station at Durrow and are met by an open-back coal lorry which takes us and our camping gear down to the campsite!

1968 Belfast to Wicklow

It's my only organised rail tour in Ireland. We travel the previous day on the last steam-hauled 'Belfast Boat Express' from Manchester to Heysham and the 'M.V. Duke of Lancaster' to Belfast. The special runs from Belfast to Dublin with an NIR tank locomotive replaced by a

CIE steam locomotive at Dublin for the trip to Wicklow and back. At a customs check at the border station of Dundalk (pictured) on the return, a nearby passenger, when asked the question *"Did you buy anything in the Republic,"* answers, *"A cup of tea."* Laughs all around and a bemused customs officer!

1978 Rosslare to Dublin and on to Galway on a train with no beer!

On the first of several journeys I make with Robert for the Ireland v Wales rugby at Rosslare, we witness train information Irish-style. Enquiring about the train to Dublin, we get an ambiguous answer *"The train to Dublin's a bus and only goes to Wexford."* On being pressed further, *"But a special train's been put on for the rugby."* We make Arklow that evening, where we stay the night. The next day after the match, we decide to travel to Galway to stay the night. The evening train from Dublin is heaving with Irish fans, who, as do the Welsh, like their beer. Wales wins 20-16, so the Irish drown their sorrows in the bar car. Then disaster; *"The bar's run out of beer,"* announces the guard as we approach Athlone *"But don't worry, I'll ask the steward on the Dublin train if he can let us have his stock. There will be some delay."* The trains cross at Athlone, so it will be easy to make a transfer. *"Good news, there's plenty of beer, but there will be a further delay while we deal with the paperwork."*

1984 Rosslare to Dun Laoghaire by road

Courtesy of the late Hugh Gould, who has just become British Rail's Manager for Wales. Hugh organises a facility visit for the passenger sales team to meet with the Irish Tourist Board to promote travel from Wales to the Republic. We start with a botched presentation by the ITB at Rosslare, the planned coach to take us to Glendalough in County Wicklow and a beauty spot called 'Meeting of the Waters' is late, and on arrival, the catering doesn't appear as it's been booked for the following day; extemporisation is the order of the day, but the rest of the trip to Dun Laoghaire including dinner and overnight stay goes well. I notice the Dublin suburban train system is at last gasp with wheezing diesel locomotives. Fortunately, electrification is on the way!

1985 Rosslare to Belfast

In December 1985, I start a consultancy assignment to provide a marketing plan for Northern Ireland Railways. I'm asked to make my initial journey to Belfast via Rosslare and Dublin to travel on NIR's flagship 'Enterprise' train. The reason is evident as I board the train at Dublin Connolly; it's old and shabby, covered with security notices and dire penalties. I must even take my luggage with me when I go to the loo! If this is the flagship, what is the rest like? I am presented with quite a task to help map a way out of this. Northern Ireland at the time of 'The Troubles' makes life challenging!

1986 Transport co-ordination (or perhaps not) in the North

Public transport is in disarray in Northern Ireland, and things can only get better! Belfast has two stations, Central and York Road; the latter is the station for the Larne and Derry lines. Publicly owned 'Citybus' doesn't remotely co-ordinate with the trains. I spend a morning peak hour in York Road, a mile from the city centre, and bus connections are provided. However, every bus leaves up to 5 minutes before each incoming train! In addition to all this, 'Ulsterbus' is in cutthroat competition with NIR and has a journey time advantage on the main Belfast to Derry route. Thankfully, those days are long past, and now, Northern Ireland enjoys a fully integrated and modern public transport network.

1993 To Galway and Ennis courtesy of Iarnrod Eireann

A pleasant duty in my latter days with British Rail is representing Wales in the 'Anglo-Irish Best Station Competition' awards. On my second such trip to Ireland in 1993, Irish Railways offers me free travel on its network, so I'm off to Galway, then on to Ennis to travel on the newly introduced Ennis to Limerick train. At Galway, I get a Bus Eireann  coach from the station. I'm approached by a burly man who looks like he's been in a fight, *"Where do I get the train to Cork?."* Getting to Cork is a bit difficult, requiring a change at Kildare, and as I am about to advise him to take the coach, he says, *"Then why de f..k have I got a ticket to Cork?"* I beat a hasty retreat! The coach journey is interesting, and everybody's chatting about some 'faux pas' by a government minister over misspending EU money. My reason for going to Ennis is for a new train introduced to and from Limerick over a line that's been closed to passengers for 25 years. I go to the station in the evening, and a coach arrives in lieu of the train from Limerick, so I'm not hopeful next morning! Through the gloom, I see steam rising from the coaches, and a train it is! I ask how it comes about, and it seems that the station master at Ennis thought they should have a train, so he organised it without consulting a higher authority. It could only happen in Ireland!

2000 Kilkenny to Dublin Heuston

Josiane and I are on holiday staying in Kilkenny and decide to take the train for our trip to Dublin to see the famous 'Book of Kells' in Trinity College. I recall a comfortable train journey with an informative guard who announces the train calling points, followed by *"and if you've got your feet on the seats, take them off!"*

It's a Long, Long Way to Achill Island

In 1967, I am touring by train in Ireland with Robert, and although we have a rough itinerary mapped out, we still get to unexpected places. It's my second only visit to the Republic though Robert has made several visits before on family holidays, and his plan to go to **Achill Island** is a complete surprise to me.

I take up the story at the sleepy country junction of Claremorris in County Mayo, where we arrive on the train from Dublin. It's the railhead for the famous shrine at Knock and its celebrated priest Monsignor James Horan who by this time has built a 10,000-capacity basilica and is to build an international airport twelve years later! Claremorris is a junction on the Dublin to Westport line with freight branches south to Athenry and northeast to Sligo. We talk to the station master, who, on learning of our desire to get to Sligo (which ordinarily would involve going back to Mullingar and then to Sligo), says he will arrange a trip for us on the direct daily freight train the next day.

Thrilled with this prospect, we travel on to Westport and catch a late afternoon bus to Achill Island. I have never heard of this place and concerned that with no bus back that evening, we could be stranded without accommodation. It turns out to be a long journey in a rickety old bus, and we cross a bridge from the mainland. The weather isn't great, so it's not the scenic delight it could be. We arrive at the village of Dooagh on the far west of the island. The modern world has passed it by, and the village is crisscrossed by rough roads – cattle and other livestock roams around freely – very exotic! We do find accommodation and have a pleasant night.

The next morning, we take the first bus out, which arrives at Westport just after the Dublin train has left, with the next one not until lunchtime. We need to get to Claremorris soon, so resort to 'thumbing'; it isn't long before a Coca-Cola van man picks us up and says he is going to Sligo. *"So are we,"* we say, but can he please drop us at Claremorris? I won't go into the distorted logic of our decision to the van driver; suffice it to say, he drops us at Claremorris thinking we are barking mad!

The lonely road on the approach to Dooagh; no way back tonight!

On our arrival at Claremorris, all is quiet save for a short freight train being prepared over in the sidings, and all seems well: it is not to be so. We seek out the station master who, on seeing us, appears distraught and, with panic in his eyes, says, *"The Sligo train's got an inspector on the engine, which means you can't go at all – but I promised you a trip, so I'll fix it with the guard."* The guard accepts on the condition that we hide under the seats when he stops to shunt en route in case the inspector walks back. The train meanders through rural Mayo, stopping to shunt wagons at sleepy villages: Swinford, Charlestown, and Tubbercurry. At each, we perform a ritual 'hiding' but see no sign of the inspector. By the time we arrive at Collooney Junction, where we join the main line from Dublin to Sligo, our guard is in panic mode, *"You can't go to Sligo, or you'll be seen by the inspector, so you get out here."*

The junction is a remote spot, and the line is on a high embankment and not far from the Northern Ireland border. We scramble down a steep embankment, find the main road, and walk into Sligo. Twelve months later and the start of 'The Troubles' and we might have been seen as escaping IRA fugitives, the mind boggles!

Sligo is the County town in the county of the same name and is obviously important. Its capacious station was the terminus for the main line from Dublin and two other lines from Claremorris and Enniskillen, both of which joined the main line at Collooney Junction. We stay the night here and return to Dublin the next day on a diesel railcar, the first of only three trains a day on this route. At that time and for many years after, the standard offering on all but the Cork and Belfast lines from Dublin is just three long-distance trains a day, a situation that continues for the next thirty years or so. Things move ever so slowly on Irish Railways!

The terminus at Sligo looking south 25 years later with a train from Dublin in the smart standard livery introduced by *IE* in the late 1980s. There are only three trains per day to and from Dublin (which has been increased substantially in recent years).

The nearside platform may well have been for the 'Sligo, Leitrim, and Northern Counties' trains which ceased as far back as 1957.

The 'County Donegal Railways' never reached as far south as Sligo.

Off to Find a Campsite on the Dingle Peninsula

A year after our trip, I catch sight of the 'M.V. Innisfallen' in a less than pristine condition in Swansea.

Some two years later, in 1969, I join scouting friend Edward on a mission to find a site for his forthcoming summer camp, which he has established is located at tiny Ballyferriter on the far west of the remote Dingle Peninsula.

We start our journey on a bus from Neath to Swansea Docks, where we are to board the first ever Swansea-Cork Ferry in the super-smart 'Innisfallen.' It is Spring Bank Holiday and unseasonably warm, so we eschew a cabin and sleep comfortably on deck in our sleeping bags. Arriving refreshed at Cobh harbour, the port for the city of Cork, we take the bus link to the city. We have a few hours and find it a very agreeable city. Our train to Tralee leaves around lunchtime and travels up the main line to Mallow, then west for an increasingly scenic ride to Killarney. It is a terminal station, and the train must reverse out and reverse yet again to gain the line to Tralee. To the south is the beautifully named 'Macgillycuddy's Reeks' range, and from here on, the line twists and turns through very spectacular countryside. At the intermediate station of Farranfore, there is a small airport for County Kerry; it was also a one-time inland junction for an exotic line to Europe's most westerly station of Valentia Harbour. Soon after, we arrive at Tralee, the line's terminus.

Our Cork to Tralee train at Killarney, a terminus station with double reversal before continuing.

Tralee is a small market town and bustling local centre for the Dingle Peninsula. Like many country towns in the Republic, it is old-fashioned, with a lot of its local commerce still done by horse and cart.

Much local trade in Tralee still relies on the horse and cart.

It was the starting point of the infamous 'Tralee and Dingle' narrow-gauge network, whose passenger trains ceased in 1939 and freight in 1953. The narrow-gauge trains have long since been replaced by buses, one of which we take on the next stage of our journey to the small town of Dingle. The road faithfully follows the line of the railway most of the way, but our old bus is much safer than the trains, which had a questionable record! We reach Dingle in the late afternoon, and booking in at a local hotel, discover we've just missed seeing some of the cast of the film

'Ryan's Daughter,' including the star John Mills. They are using the hotel as their base and have gone away for a holiday. We are to see many props for this film on our journey the next day.

In the morning, we hire bikes for the final stage of our journey (it now being the fourth mode of transport used). It's a leisurely and bucolic ride along the coast road where we come to a film set village, an authentic-looking place complete with church, pub, etc., until we look behind only to find it's just a façade! We later spot networks of ropes and pulleys presumably used to get film gear to the beach below. Shortly after, we spot a basking shark, a first for me. Across Dingle Bay are the Blasket Islands, amazingly beautiful in azure-blue waters, and beyond is the Atlantic Ocean. We veer north on the end of the peninsula and drop down into the tiny village of Ballyferriter. Edward is delighted after such a long and challenging journey to arrive at this paradise and decides to book the camp site with no further ado. We cycle back to Dingle and the reverse of our outward journey; the ferry is a daytime sailing to Swansea, and the weather has reverted to rain!

Ballyferriter, one of the most beautiful places on the west coast

The Delights of County Donegal

An idyllic scene greets me in the late afternoon at Rossnowlagh, County Donegal.

County Donegal, straddling the northwest and north coasts of the Republic, is at one point north of Northern Ireland. It's a part of Ireland that I've longed to go to, and as it's very difficult to do by public transport, I must wait until I make a car trip. This comes in late November 1990 when I take a few days off work, get into my Ford Mondeo (yes, I was a 'Mondeo man' once!), and head for the afternoon sailing of Stena ferry 'M.V. Felicity' at Fishguard. Despite the time of year, it's a smooth crossing, and I check into a nice hotel overlooking the sea in Rosslare.

The weather is excellent the next day, and I leave early with the intention to reach Donegal by nightfall. Crossing Ireland transversely, there aren't many good roads (must have been rolled by a steamroller with a hump!), but it's a pleasant journey through Counties Wexford, Carlow, and Laoise and I stop for lunch at Portlaoise. From there on to Athlone, I become a casualty of odd Irish road signage but manage to get back on track as I strike north through Roscommon to Sligo. In this section, the road crosses the Dublin-Sligo railway line at Boyle;

I consult the train timetable and find a train is due shortly, set myself up in a large field, and get a cracking shot of the train. Then I spot a bull in the far corner and walk carefully back to the gate, vaulting over in panic as the bull advances. Rather shaken, I continue my journey without further incident. I don't have time to stop over in Sligo as it is late afternoon, and there's a great deal to fit in before sunset. I visit the famous poet W B Yeats' grave in a church below one of Ireland's most prominent mountains, 'Benbulben.' The road is now on the coast and the next town, Ballyshannon, is an unremarkable seaside resort though from here on, it just gets better. The low sun is an aid to good photography, and I become so mesmerised by the amazingly beautiful scene at Rossnowlagh looking across Donegal Bay that I linger for half an hour.

The afternoon Sligo to Dublin train near Boyle, Co. Roscommon.

I aim to arrive at Donegal town before dark and am glad I do. After checking in at a small hotel, I wander down to the harbour just in time to see a magical sunset. What is it about this place – I can't get over how beautiful it is – and there's more to come! I get some dinner in the hotel and settle down to an evening's TV (with 'Gaelic' subtitles).

A gorgeous sunset over the harbour in Donegal town.

Next morning, I'm up early as I need to get back to Rosslare by nightfall, though by a very different route. First, I seek out traces of the famous 'County Donegal Railway (CDR)', a narrow-gauge network that stretched out extensively in the surrounding area but find little apart from the old station. I drive along the coast road to the attractive village of Killybegs (terminus of a CDR branch line) before heading north to Ardara, an ordinary village that is extraordinarily picturesque in a strange sort of way with curling wisps of smoke from home peat fires.

My route now turns west and follows the former *CDR* line through Glenties and Stranorlar, both well-known stations in days of yore. The road reaches the border between the Republic and the North at Lifford, crossing the river Foyle into Strabane. Though I had been in the North as recently as 1986 on consultancy work, I am quite unprepared for the horrors of this town with its general air of menace, so I don't stop and hastily drive south, finding the next town of Omagh much more agreeable. My final call in the North is to be at Fintona, a place that once had a horse-drawn tram to Fintona Junction (the horse's name was 'Dick,' thought you'd like to know!). Of this, there is no trace, and though I stop for lunch, I am uncomfortable with dire warnings to *"Check your car carefully"* before leaving. I look up my map to find the

Ardara in County Donegal.

best route back to Rosslare and choose what appears to be a relatively straightforward route, west to Enniskillen, then on a trunk road running south-east via Cavan and Navan to the Dublin suburbs; it's long and tedious, slightly relieved by a newly opened motorway from Dublin towards Carlow, whereupon it peters out into the bumpy road I used on my outward journey. A very tired me arrives at Rosslare in time for dinner and a good night's sleep before taking the 09:00 ferry to Fishguard the next morning.

Round the Ring of Kerry

A panoramic view of Valentia Island, a wilder setting one could not imagine. The railway terminated at Valentia Harbour on the mainland (foreground) though there is no trace.

A year later, I make another road trip to the west of Ireland, this time with Paul and Peter and earlier in the autumn. The sea journey is again via Fishguard-Rosslare and an overnight stay in Rosslare.

This year, our objective is the famous and picturesque Ring of Kerry and a personal desire of mine to see the site of the one-time westernmost railway station in Europe at Valentia Harbour. From Rosslare, we head west, the road going well north of the railway to Waterford, avoiding deep sea inlets which the railway crosses on bridges. At New Ross, I see the former 'Bellport' container terminal, which used to receive ships from Newport which travelled up the tidal river Barrow. It's a long journey, so we don't linger and pass Waterford, taking our lunch break at Clonmel. Here, the road heads deep into the mountainous territory before dropping down to Mallow, where we cross the Dublin to Cork railway.

The road from Mallow to Killarney follows the railway I travelled on my 1969 trip to Tralee. We pass through Millstreet which is to achieve fame in 1993 when it hosts the Eurovision song contest, the only Irish venue outside Dublin to achieve this distinction. We stay in Killarney and find it a most agreeable town, in line with its reputation for beauty and as the centre for the famed 'Ring of Kerry' road. At the hotel, we find it odd to see that people are watching a TV programme broadcast in the Gaelic tongue with Gaelic-looking subtitles. Thinking it's just one of those Irish 'quirks', we are surprised to find there is a 'Kerry Gaelic', with some similarities to the national version.

We are in for a real treat as we set out on the 'Ring of Kerry' heading along the peninsula with Dingle Bay to the north of us. Today's weather, cloudy and wet, precludes seeing the bay to my best advantage, so I content myself with memories of years earlier on the Dingle Peninsula when the weather was a lot better. Neither do we get a good view of some of the highest mountains in Ireland. By late morning, we are at Cahirciveen and take a road signposted Valentia Island. I am full of anticipation that we will see traces of the most westerly station in Europe at the end of what was claimed to be Ireland's most spectacular railway from Farranfore. Valentia, in the mid-19th century, was a town of 2000 people and famous for having the first ever trans-Atlantic cable coming ashore there. It's downhill for the railway as the population dwindles to 600 with little railway traffic. Valentia Harbour station opens in 1893 and lasts until 1960. This is a wild and beautiful place, and I would have loved the train journey!

The main street in Kenmare, the principal town on the 'Ring of Kerry' route.

We proceed around the west coast of the peninsula, then turn east along the north shore of the Kenmare River to the town of Kenmare, one of its principal settlements. Due to the poor weather, it's been a hard drive, so we stop here and stay the night. It is a lively and attractive little town, by now an important tourist destination. How changed it is compared to places I visit twenty or so years before when horsepower is the order of the day.

The next day, we travel over the most spectacular parts of the peninsula, where the road twists and turns continuously, revealing coast and mountain vistas in profusion. One is Bantry Bay, one of the deepest harbours in Europe and the site of a major oil terminal with a rather chequered history. We continue to Skibbereen, another place with a quirky railway history. A junction on the 'Cork, Bandon, and South Coast Railway' to Bantry and Baltimore once hosted the narrow-gauge 'Skull and Skibbereen Tramway' closed as early as 1952, nine years before the closure of the CB&SC. From here on, the road has a gentler profile and runs some way inland, though we make a small diversion to the attractive resort of Kinsale, of interest to me as it's twinned with Mumbles.

The stunning coastline at Stradbally, near Dungarvan, County Waterford.

We pass through Cork, then via Youghal, famous for its carpets, and Dungarvan (my first destination in Ireland). The road surmounts fearsome gradients and has recently been rebuilt as a dual carriageway that blasts its way through the rocks to create an even gradient – most impressive! The direct railway from Dungarvan to Cork via Cappoquin closed in the late 1960s; I travelled on it far as Dungarvan in 1966 en route to a scout camp.

We return to Rosslare, staying overnight at Waterford, and take the Rosslare-Fishguard ferry back to Wales.

Rosslare to Limerick   Ireland's Most Interesting Train Journey

Once the main line for boat trains from Rosslare to Cork, this railway has gradually and irrevocably been downgraded or closed completely. My first trip in 1966 from Rosslare to Dungarvan is a high spot of my journeys, and my last through run from Limerick Junction to Rosslare is in 1993. Early in the present century, this part of the line is shut completely after a short period carrying only freight.

The railway route is moderately scenic throughout and passes through the mountainous country towards its western end. The first part, from Rosslare to Waterford, is along coastal marshes, the sea making deep indentations, forcing the railway to bridge them with some very fine structures. The main road is well north, and consequently, settlements are small. This part closes to passengers not long after my last trip but remains for several years for freight (sugar beet) from factories at Wellingtonbridge. The largest viaduct spans the tidal river Barrow just before we get into Waterford Plunkett, a substantial station in a waterside location some way from the city. Leaving here, the main line to Dublin diverges west of the station, with the former line to Mallow a little further on.

Waterford is the largest settlement on the route, and its Plunkett station, so named as are many other Irish stations after a local leader in the 1916 'Easter Rising.' Connection is made here with Intercity services to and from Dublin (of which there are just four per day). A late afternoon arrival from Dublin is pictured behind one of the General Motors 141 class passenger diesel locomotives, ubiquitous in the Republic at that time (October 1993).

The line west from Waterford (still open with limited service) serves the substantial towns of Carrick on Suir and Clonmel, with the countryside more undulating, and after Cahir, climbs into the Galty Mountains. To the north is the 'Rock of Cashel' once the seat of Irish Kings, one of whom, it is said, changed sides several times from a Protestant king to a Roman Catholic bishop, depending on which was in the ascendancy at the time. Soon we are at famous Tipperary, quite a modest town, allegedly 'a long way' from anywhere!

Limerick Junction station is the most bizarre I have ever seen. At the time of my visit, every train on the Dublin-Cork main line must reverse into its single through platform. The movements of Limerick to Waterford trains are subject to no less than three reversals. Arriving from Limerick, they come round the back of the station and reverse into the bay platform *(photo)*; then pull forward, reverse towards Limerick, then a final reversal before moving on across the entire main line. Confused? I am!

Limerick Junction station is the most bizarre I have ever seen. At the time of my visit, every train on the Dublin-Cork main line must reverse into its single through platform. The movements of Limerick to Waterford trains are subject to no less than three reversals. Arriving from Limerick, they come round the back of the station and reverse into the bay platform *(photo)*; then pull forward, reverse towards Limerick, then a final reversal before moving on across the entire main line. Confused? I am!

Shortly after, the train arrives at Limerick Junction after crossing the main line on the level, then reversing into the station. The station has the most bizarre track/platform layout imaginable (see above)! The final 10 miles to Limerick Colbert has a regular shuttle connecting to and from Dublin and Cork and travels through unremarkable country to arrive at a substantial terminus station at Limerick.

The famous 'Waverley' Paddle Steamer is totally at home *'doon the water'* in Rothesay, Isle of Bute.

Scotland is a country I get to know very well, and though recent visits have been to lowland regions. I go to pretty well every part of the Highlands and Islands over the years. Some visits are extreme in various ways, but all are thoroughly enjoyable, and I see the most amazing places.

In the ensuing pages, you can follow several of my journeys of adventure by train, car, and ship to the uttermost ends of the Highlands and Islands and several anecdotes of travel by train in Scotland.

Getting to some of these remote places is difficult but is made easier up to the late 1980s by a unique publication illustrated here. It is packed with information on how to get almost anywhere, even down to phone numbers to ring for a boatman to take you to a remote island. It really makes travel simpler!

Travelling Around Scotland by Train

Early morning in Stranraer, and the Carlisle local is ready to depart.

On my first visit in 1960, the rail network is still quite extensive and being unable to predict even the near future, I wish I had covered more lines. I particularly miss Dunblane to Crianlarich (Callander & Oban), the northeast Scotland lines from Aberdeen to Fraserburgh and Peterhead; and from Gleneagles to Comrie and Crieff. I do manage the Borders (Edinburgh to Carlisle) and Dumfries to Stranraer, both of which become casualties of Beeching.

Despite this, there is much left to see, and over the years, I cover virtually the entire network. In a recent and more enlightened age, lines are reopened, and I manage to catch up with them. The largest is the Borders Line running from Edinburgh to Tweedbank, and one where I am invited to do some marketing consultancy on the re-opening, so I'm proud to travel by train to the Borders again in 2015. Inevitably, given the amount of time I spend in Scotland, it's difficult to cover everything in detail, so I take several highlights of what I term 'travel adventures,' for that is what they are.

I make other epic journeys in Scotland, notably with Robert in 1965, when we cover a large area and include such gems as the Aberfeldy branch, the secondary route from Aviemore to Forres, and the original main line between Perth and Montrose via Forfar. In 1976, I book a wildlife holiday in Glen Affric. In a week of cool and changeable weather in an otherwise blazing summer, I climb two mountains in Strathglass (one is a 'Munro') and fail to spot a golden eagle; yet perversely, on my visit the following week to Oban by train, sitting on the fence by the line in the Pass of Brander is an eagle! A few days later, I'm on paddle steamer

'Waverley' *'doon the watter'* from Glasgow to Rothesay, changing to turbine steamer, 'Queen Mary' from there to Largs.

Another visit takes me to Tongue and Durness in Sutherland, Tobermory in Mull (famed as 'Balamory' on children's TV), and a trip on a steamer to Coll and Tiree (previously known only to me as a 'sea area' on the shipping forecast). And many more visits to the cities of Edinburgh and Glasgow, both of which are firm favourites.

One of my best trips is on the Far North line to Thurso in 1963. At Kildonan,
the southbound 'Orcadian' passes.

A Scottish Rail Miscellany

On my first visit to Scotland, I stay with Peter in Edinburgh. We share a common interest in trains and make several trips together. One is to Glasgow, the main purpose being to visit engine sheds, but I also want to see the iconic electric new 'Blue Trains' on the north Clyde lines. A week before, there has been a major electrical fault, the fleet is withdrawn, and steam trains resume. It is some years later that I see these trains in service on the south Clyde lines.

How I come to be on a train at Alloa in November 2008 is a story in itself. I am off to York for a Community Rail conference and decide to fly to Newcastle (a route I've never done). With no available seats from Cardiff, I look up BMI Baby's offering to Edinburgh. On my screen comes *"one seat remaining at £1 plus taxes on the 0645 hrs*

flight." So, I book, get up very early, arrive in Edinburgh at 08:00, travel to Alloa and Larkhall, sample new train services, then a GNER train Glasgow to York, arrive knackered that evening!

An unexpected bonus of my epic 48-hour visit with Hugh to Aberdeen and back in 1963 is several hours in Glasgow on the return trip. We cross to St Enoch station to find its local services are still 50% steam operated. Most trains are hauled by standard Class 4 tank and tender locomotive types. The real surprise is when a local, long-distance train from Carlisle arrives behind a scruffy run-down 'Princess Coronation,' relegated from top-line duties.

Up to the mid-1960s, it is still possible to find fascinating branch lines all over Scotland, but the 'Beeching' clear-out is much more ruthless than elsewhere, and by the middle of the decade, very few remain (and soon to go). Robert and I chance upon the attractive branch to Aberfeldy, which leaves the Perth to Inverness line at

Ballinluig. With a BRCW diesel locomotive and one carriage, even this is too much as we are the only passengers!

1963 South Wales to Northern Scotland and back in 48 hours

Our train for Aberdeen waits to depart from Glasgow Buchanan Street station.

I am indebted to my friend, Hugh, who compiled a detailed log of this trip.

Hugh and I are railwaymen in Swansea in 1963 when we're challenged by two (also railwaymen) friends in Newport to see who can get the furthest distance in 48 hours using our free rail passes.

Our A3 Pacific stops at Perth for water .

We map out a route that will take us to Aberdeen and back with enough time to cover the branch line to Ballater on Deeside. We start from Swansea Victoria at 1830 hrs on the 'York Mail' over the Central Wales line to Shrewsbury and on to Crewe. We change to a diesel-hauled overnight London-Glasgow train which is very crowded and share a compartment with two unsavoury-looking characters who insist on taking their shoes off and stinking the place out! Our arrival at Glasgow Central is at an unearthly hour in the morning; we grab some breakfast and cross to Buchanan Street, and it's back to steam traction for the train through to Aberdeen. This is a fast train routed over the Forfar route, but not yet on a three-hour schedule (Chapter 9). We have several hours at Aberdeen before our return train and find we can get to Ballater and back in that time. It is the heart of Royal Deeside and railhead for Balmoral Castle, but we rule out going to see the Queen today. Back in Aberdeen, we see our train to Glasgow waiting with an A3 Pacific (same type as the 'Flying Scotsman'), and there is a good turn of speed with a heavy train. It's a lovely evening, and we enjoy the great scenery of the east coast before arriving at Perth for a water stop. On our arrival at Glasgow, we have several hours to kill before our overnight train to Crewe, so we take a local train to Neilston and back to rack up our miles. The Euston train from here is lightly loaded, so we have plenty of space to stretch out on the seats and sleep fitfully. A bonus: our locomotive is a steam 'Coronation' class 'City of Stoke on Trent' not yet ousted by a diesel, and at Crewe, I manage a photo in the early morning light. A last effort to further rack up miles sees us on a side trip to Liverpool, coming back on a heavily loaded 'Shamrock' hauled by a new electric locomotive. Back to Cardiff with a steam 'Castle' class and finally a 'Hymek' diesel to Neath. When we tot up our mileage back in Neath, we've beaten the others by a short head! (1278 miles).

1970: A Travelling and Hostelling Adventure to the Western Isles

The herring fishing boats are back in harbour at Mallaig, and we are offered as much as we want – free.

In Chapter 7, I write about my adventurous journeys to Scotland for mountaineering. A year on from my trip to Wester Ross in 1969, I am in the same part of Scotland on another less arduous outdoor activity, youth hostelling with some walking. I am accompanied by a friend who is a keen hosteller.

I travel up to the capital to meet my friend, and we take an overnight train from London Euston to Inverness, a journey of 517 miles. Starting with an electric locomotive, the train switches over to diesel power at Crewe. On our arrival at Inverness the next morning, we are soon on a Kyle of Lochalsh train and ride one of Scotland's most spectacular routes, alighting at the remote station of Achnasheen, where a bus is waiting. This is no ordinary bus; this one conveys mail, livestock, etc., as well as a few passengers. Some are known to our driver, who tells me he's been doing this run for 35 years and knows his regular customers. *"Good*

Gairloch, where we alight and take an 'exotic' bus to the hostel.

day madam, you'll be Mrs McPherson, home from New Zealand. Your sister will be meeting you at the crossroads," is his greeting to a lady boarding with a suitcase. The schedule is flexible and when we ask the driver if there's time to buy refreshments at the Achnasheen Hotel, it's *"och aye, just tell me when you want to go!"* We stay on the bus until Gairloch, where there is an hour to wait before another very unusual bus – it carries the groceries and household items to those living along the route to Melvaig – and we alight at Carn Dearg youth hostel five miles down the road; it's small in a stunning location by Loch Gairloch which is basic and friendly.

The next day, we are up early for the bus leaves at 08:45 and there is an hour's wait at Gairloch for the post bus back to Achnasheen and the train to Kyle of Lochalsh. We are faced with a problem; it's a Saturday, the 'Sabbath' is the following day, and no hostels on Skye are open. There's a hostel on the island of Raasay, which is open though there is no Sunday ferry. We take ferry 'Loch Arkaig' from Kyle

Achnasheen and our train for Kyle arriving.

to Raasay, and it's three miles to the hostel, which we walk. We stay two nights there with not much to do on Sunday except take a walk around the island.

Monday morning and another three-mile hike to the quayside in the pouring rain only to find that the ferry is over an hour late; the quay is totally exposed, so we get very wet. The 'Loch Arkaig' arrives and departs with a lot of passengers, and once on the open sea, lists in the wind through 45 degrees, an exhilarating, lively trip to Kyle of Lochalsh! Fortunately, the weather clears which is just as well as that afternoon we are to take the 'Loch Seaforth,' a traditional steamer, to Stornoway on Lewis, which must negotiate the notorious 'Minch' sea channel. It stays fine and sunny, and we spend a lot of time on deck. They serve a Scottish high tea in the restaurant with crisp linen tablecloths and a white-jacketed waiter, some real old-fashioned service!

The 'Loch Seaforth' at Stornoway, this night it will host a very special passenger!

Arrival in Stornoway is in the early evening after a four-hour voyage, and we book into a nice B&B, there being no hostels on Lewis. Later in the evening, we hear the sound of bagpipes and wonder what it's all about. A pipe band is marching to the harbour, and when we arrive it is clear they are piping the first ever Scottish Nationalist MP, Donald Stewart, on board en route to his first session in Westminster, where he will arrive 36 hours later! Though not remotely a nationalist, I feel honoured to be there. Stornoway is the main centre in Lewis with its own small bus network, heading to settlements on the north and west coasts of the island, one of which is called 'Back'! There are no buses the next day to the south (which is known as Harris even though it's on the same island). Thus, we resort to thumbing lifts, and it takes a long time before someone stops; as well as no buses, there is very little other road traffic! The van driver takes us to Tarbert, from where it is a modest walk through stunning scenery to our next hostel at Stockinish. This turns out to be an ultra-remote spot on the Rodel peninsula.

Only one other person is in the hostel, a semi-permanent resident who is a writer and a real 'fruitcake' with it, and she bores us rigid with her ramblings. In all other respects, it's the perfect setting for getting away from it all, and we reflect the joy of having reached the outermost settled island of Scotland. Nearby is the experimental village of Leverburgh, set up by Lord Lever to develop fisheries in this remote area; it all came to grief! We leave the next day and walk back to Tarbert for the midday car ferry 'Hebrides' to Uig on the north coast of Skye. There is at least a bus here that takes us to Portree, the principal town on the island and quite a bustling little place. Another takes us down the east coast of the island to yet another ferry from Armadale to Mallaig, the 'Clansman.' Most of the ferries we use are run by MacBrayne's, which, though providing a vital lifeline, are reviled for their high prices.

The idyllic view from our youth hostel at Stockinish on Harris.

Mallaig is an interesting place with many trawlers landing herring, and there is lots of activity in selling and despatching the fish. I ask if I can buy two herrings for supper, and we are thrown a few and invite to take what we want, gratis! I pack the fish into a bag and decide to eat them the following night. Then we take the train the short distance to Morar and stay the night in its youth hostel.

Turbine steamer 'King George V' arriving at Fort William.

Morar is a very attractive village, and much as we would like to stay on, we must leave the next day on the West Highland train for an amazing scenic ride to Fort William. Here, as we arrive, so does turbine steamer 'King George V'! We have lunch in Fort William and take the afternoon Glasgow train, where we plan to alight at Corrour; it's Britain's highest (and most remote) station, for its equally remote hostel at Loch Ossian. We are the only ones to get off the train and are faced with a bleak but beautiful landscape. There is no road link to the outside world, just a rough track out of the station, and we walk a mile to the hostel, a small wooden building on the edge of the loch. On the door, a scribbled note says the warden has gone off to Glasgow for the night and to make ourselves at home.

After settling in, we unpack the fish from Mallaig and cook a fine supper. There is a large country house at the other end of the loch, but it is derelict and burnt out, so we are quite alone. We at least get a good night's sleep – the only noise in the early morning is the rattling of a distant diesel locomotive – and are fresh to resume our journey. This is over the wild and beautiful Rannoch Moor, backed by high mountains. Later, to the east is Loch Lomond, and on the west, Loch Long and Gareloch (with its nuclear submarine base at Faslane). We pass through the western suburbs to arrive at Queen Street station in Glasgow. We cross the city to the central station and our through train to London Euston.

Wild and beautiful, quite the most remote place I've ever stayed: the lonely track from Corrour to Loch Ossian youth hostel.

1973: A Road Travel Adventure in the Highlands

The iconic Eilean Donan Castle, rebuilt in authentic style in the 19th century, is near Kyle of Lochalsh.

This motoring trip starts on the train as Brian's car is loaded onto the Crewe to Inverness 'Car Sleeper' train. There is anxiety as it is driven away at Crewe to be loaded into a covered van, but all is well when we see it at Inverness the next morning. It's nice to wake up in the Highlands and have a light breakfast delivered to our cabin whilst approaching Aviemore.

From Inverness it's all by road, including the journey home. We leave the city on the road to Loch Ness and travel down on the west shore of the Loch, keeping an eye out for anything resembling a monster. Even as we stop for a roadside picnic, we see nothing of interest, a rather futile exercise given there has only been a handful of sightings in 50 or so years! We turn inland at Drumnadrochit to visit the beautiful and well-known Glen Affric which is on a narrow minor road, then to Glen Mullardoch and the loch of the same name before returning to Loch Ness. Here, we drive west through a landscape of some very impressive mountain ranges on both sides and arrive at Strathcarron and the beautiful village of Plockton, where we stay in a B&B for a couple of eventful days. The village and loch, it seems, are under threat from a proposal to build oil platforms off Drumbuie lower down the loch, and feelings are running high; the American prospectors are not welcome, especially as they insist on calling the place 'Drambuie!' On our first evening, we are told about a 'Ceilidh' (Highland folk dance) in the village hall that evening, which is being televised live for BBC's 'Nationwide' programme, the money raised to go to the fighting fund. Brian and I go along, and it's the most incredible event I've seen; literally, everyone is there, from lairds to crofters in all styles of dress, and I am filmed (and appear on TV) doing the 'eightsome reel.' It's great fun and goes on into the early hours.

View looking north over Loch Ness from Invermoriston.

At breakfast the next morning, I am intrigued by what appears on my plate to be a light brown burger along with poached eggs. With a glint in her eye, the landlady tells me, *"That's haggis."* It's my first experience of haggis, and I like it very much. After breakfast, we drive up

The impressive Falls of Measach in the mist.

Loch Carron parallel to the Kyle of Lochalsh railway line, then off towards Ullapool. Not far short of Ullapool, we visit Corrieshalloch Gorge and one of Scotland's most spectacular waterfalls, the 'Falls of Measach,' which drop over 150 feet into the valley. High above us is 'Beinn Dearg' (3560 feet), one of Scotland's most spectacular 'Munros' which today is shrouded in cloud. We move on to Ullapool – the new terminus of the car ferry to Stornoway – before returning to Plockton. The next day, we take a short trip on a train to Duirinish, the next stop towards Kyle, and walk back. We view the site of the proposed oil platforms and agree it will be criminal if they go ahead (they don't). Later, we continue our journey and take a lonely road to the very beautiful village of Glenelg, which has been on my mind after discovering it's the secret place in the book 'Ring of Bright Water' by Gavin Maxwell about bringing up otters in a remote highland village. After his death in the late 60s, its location is revealed as this idyllic spot. From here, we travel on to Fort William with the intention of climbing Ben Nevis; we go back to the Great Glen and Loch Lochy, arriving at Fort William in the late afternoon. Following our conquest of Ben Nevis (Chapter 7), the highest mountain in Britain, the rest of the trip may seem to be an anti-climax; it is not to be so.

Idyllic Glenelg on the remote West Coast.

Fort William is at the head of Loch Linnhe, and the road to Ballachulish runs along the east bank of the loch for ten miles with great views of the Morvern peninsula. Since my 1969 trip on this road, a new bridge has been built over the mouth of Loch Leven, cutting out the massive switchback 15-mile detour route via Kinlochleven. We stay the night in Ballachulish and drive out in the evening on the road towards Oban and witness a dramatic sunset over Morvern.

This is our last day in the Highlands as we drive down towards Glasgow through the Pass of Glencoe, along the banks of Loch Lomond, and cross the Clyde on the recently opened Kingston Bridge, which avoids the city. It is then a long and tedious drive down the A74, M6, and M5 back to South Wales, broken only by a refreshment stop in what appears to be 'a pub with no beer' in the upper Clyde Valley. Another great Highland holiday!

1989: A Crazy Way to Get to Edinburgh

This is what we wake up to as the sleeper from Euston crosses bleak Rannoch Moor.

It is around 400 miles from Neath to Edinburgh, and on our trip to the Rugby International at Murrayfield in January 1989, Robert and I succeed in stretching this to a journey of no less than 1500 miles via London, Glasgow, Mallaig, Kyle of Lochalsh, Thurso, Wick, Inverness, and Perth. Not only that but in addition to the trains, we travel on two ferries and two buses. How crazy is that?

The journey starts in earnest when we board the overnight sleeper from London Euston to Fort William. I've done this journey several times, and I'm always bowled over waking up around bleak Rannoch Moor and enjoy a good breakfast in the dining car; sheer luxury! It's a pity that it's a poor year for snow and the magic of a white moor eludes us. The sleeper arrives at Fort William around mid-morning in time to connect to the train to Mallaig over the West Highland extension, considered to be the best railway journey in Britain. In summer, there's the 'Jacobite' steam train, but in winter, it's a diesel. The scenery stays the same and is arguably more beautiful than in summer.

At Mallaig, we take a ferry to Armadale in Skye. Today, the 'M.V. Lochmor' is going on to the islands of Eigg, Rhum, and Muck, and we see a large trunk destined for Rhum marked for its owner Mr Guinness. Presumably, he's on board, and likely he owns Rhum, striking us as hilariously funny! The island bus ride to Kyleakin is operated by MacBrayne's, which is notorious for its high prices though our driver is not amused when we say we are buying a journey, not the bus! The service is likely provided for residents; its passengers are two Welshmen, two Australians, and an Argentinian. The journey is very scenic, and we soon arrive in Kyleakin for the vehicle ferry over to Kyle of Lochalsh and stay the night. The Australians are also at the hotel, and we join them over dinner. They hoped to be off to Edinburgh the next day but must go on to Newcastle as no accommodation is available in the city. They are understandably puzzled, and we confirm it's down to the international rugby match.

Mallaig is the furthest west one can travel by train in Scotland, has four regular passenger trains per day plus the 'Jacobite' excursions in season. At the time of our visit, there is some freight traffic in the carriage of fish in refrigerated 'Interfrigo' wagons (left in picture). It proves uneconomical to carry this traffic which ceases soon after.

Next morning, we have time to look around Kyle before taking the 11:10 train to Inverness. It is hauled by a Class 37 diesel, now standard for Highland services. It is a journey of just under three hours through incredibly beautiful scenery. At Achnasheen, we see the postbus still meets the train, but no doubt the driver on my 1970 journey is long retired. At Dingwall, we join the Far North line, and it's now a short hop into Inverness but too late for a train to take us to Wick in daylight, so we book a hotel. With a free afternoon, we take a ride as far as Keith and back on the Aberdeen line. It is a pleasant trip through whisky country and no mountains except the Cairngorms to the south. The service has been improved with larger locomotives and faster schedules.

A busy mid-morning scene at Inverness with our Far North train (left)
and arrival from Kyle of Lochalsh (right).

The following day, we take the mid-morning train to Thurso, a 161-mile journey that takes four hours having to make two big detours to avoid estuaries. We are not concerned as there is so much scenic variety on the route to keep us interested as it hugs a wild, beautiful coast for much of the journey. In the small town of Lairg, we see a fleet of postbuses that connect the train to remote locations on the west coast. From here, it's through the Duke of Sutherland's estate with its private station, followed by a wild coastal strip to Helmsdale and finally wild peat bog known as 'Flow Country.'

At Georgemas Junction, we change to a local to Thurso, and the main train continues to Wick. There's enough time for us to look around this most northerly town in the British Isles before a bus ride across to Wick (sadly not via John o' Groats) for the evening train south. Wick, a busy fishing port, is similar in size to Thurso though we find it significantly busier. Our journey back is in fading light as far as Golspie and in darkness from there on, but it's a clear sky. We get some magical views of the sea and remote beaches and a welcome buffet serving genuine Scottish snacks, including Aberdeen Angus beef rolls. Our final day in the Highlands is on the 'Highland Chieftain', an Intercity 125 train through to London King's Cross. Running via Aviemore, Pitlochry, and Perth, arrival in Edinburgh in good time for kick-off.

Thurso, end of the line and the most northerly station in the UK, photo taken in 1963.

The Borders Line: Pre-Closure and Post Re-Opening

The railway through the Scottish Borders, from Edinburgh to Carlisle, becomes a celebrity in its own right. Proposed for closure by 'Dr Beeching', it survives until 1969 due to the weight of objections. South of Hawick is sparsely populated country, and the line is deemed surplus as there is a parallel route further west via Carstairs. I manage to travel the line in May 1965 on its one daily express train, the 'Waverley,' which travels over the original Midland Railway route from Edinburgh via Carlisle, Leeds, and Leicester to London St Pancras. It is hauled by a 'Crompton' diesel locomotive with ten coaches, and I take it as far as Carlisle.

It is with some surprise that a decision of the Scottish Parliament early this century is to restore and rebuild the route to an unspecified place in the Borders, and planning goes ahead, consultants recommending a line from Edinburgh to Tweedbank, a distance of 34 miles, of which 30 miles is a completely new track. This report is challenged by 'Borders Rail Futures', who are funded for another consultancy project on which I am co-opted to help to develop a strategy for future tourism on the line. I spend several days in the Borders in March 2004 researching prospects and pleased that some of my recommendations are in the final plan. I have an interesting response from the CEO of Borders Tourism about the potential for visitors by train to 'Sir Walter Scott' country; she simply couldn't imagine how to market this as they hadn't had trains for over 40 years!

In 2015 the new line is opened to great fanfare with a half-hourly daytime service and a programme of special steam trains. In October, Josiane and I travel from Edinburgh to Galashiels, take a bus to Melrose – where we had stayed on my consultancy visit – then back to Tweedbank and the train to Edinburgh. As we wait for the bus at Melrose, three pensioners on free bus passes are returning to Edinburgh; the driver says they will arrive there an hour earlier if they get out at Tweedbank and on the train, so they do (and they must pay for the tickets)!

Tweedbank train at Edinburgh, note the large number of passengers.

Tweedbank terminus, the train on the left is stabled having broken down early in the day.

It doesn't cross my mind as a youngster that I will be driven into climbing the highest mountains in Wales, Scotland, and England, but as soon as I get on to the high ground in my own country, it becomes an objective. However, I don't achieve the highest of all, Ben Nevis in Scotland, until I am 30 years of age; the highest in Wales, Snowdon, until I am 55; and Scafell Pike in England eludes me still despite a valiant attempt in 1967 due to very bad weather.

The mighty Ben Nevis, conquered in 1973.

Complementing my love of trains and travel is an enthusiasm for outdoor life, particularly walking and mountaineering. I inherit a love of walking from my parents, and this develops into a general interest in the outdoors, fostered by scouts and camping. The years up to my late teens are spent in the small town of Neath, surrounded on three sides by mountains with the Brecon Beacons not far beyond. In the scouts, I travel long distances to summer camps. The first in 1954, to Windermere in the Lake District. Wow! The mountains there take my breath away!

It's surprising that I find myself among the few in Neath who enjoy the outdoors and mountains. In my early teens, I bag my first mountain, the local 'March Hywel' in the Vale of Neath, followed closely by 'Craig-y-Llyn' at the top of the valley. By the early 1960s, I am actively leading groups of scouts on expeditions in the Vale of Neath and later to 'Pen-y-Fan,' the highest peak in the Brecon Beacons.

Close to the Great Tower campsite, this is the view looking over Lake Windermere towards the Langdale Fells.

Lakeside station in the 1950s (*W A Camwell*)

Curiosity and challenge describe my actions from an early age, and this trait comes to the fore on my Windermere camping trip when I plead with the leaders to take us on the lake steamers. When they refuse, I decide I will go anyway (I am 11 years of age!); on a circumnavigation of the lake, I discover new places, foremost being Lakeside station on the west bank, where three steam trains are simmering away in the station. There's a big row on my return to camp coupled with admiration of my determination! I will return to the Lake District in a later chapter of my train journeys through England. Meanwhile, come on a journey of mountaineering, fell walking and other serious outdoor pursuits starting in the early 1960s with my exploration of 'Waterfall Country' in the Vale of Neath, followed by the ascent of mountains in Scotland in the second half of the decade.

I am preparing at the time to deal with the challenges of the mountains learning climbing and abseiling skills, carried out on Dinas Rock in Pontneddfechan. Walking in 'Waterfall Country' is as good a place as any to prepare for more adventurous pursuits; the river system is complex and difficult to navigate and needs a range of skills to explore; I become a pioneer in the pursuit of extreme gorge walking, now a mainstream adventure activity. One of the waterfalls, 'Scwd Einon Gan', is a real devil to get to when I lead a group of teenagers but is well worth the effort. I have explored this entire river system and led numerous expeditions.

Scŵd Einon Gan', a most challenging waterfall.

From small beginnings come greater achievements, and on later pages, you are invited to join me on my journeys to the Highlands of Scotland, the Lakes, the Peak District, and Mid and North Wales.

The Scottish Rover Scout Challenge — 24 hours/40 miles/3 *Munros*

'Glas Tulaichen,' our third and final 'Munro,' where we experience the surreal feeling of total silence!
(Lis Burke).

This may not sound as fearsome as the real thing. Every year in the 1960s and beyond, the Scottish Scout Association organises a tough mountain contest open to Rover Scouts from all over the UK. My own group in Neath takes part in the 1965 and 1966 challenges, and two friends and I are in the 1965 team. Our leader, the local RC parish priest, loans his car – a Mini – in which his brother drives us the 400 miles to Falkirk, where we spend the night on the floor of a friend's house. The mind boggles as to how a 'Mini' with four people and a roof rack full of gear gets all that way in a day! We are threatened with being booked for parking in Lancaster; the warden, the local Scout Commissioner, lets us off.

We sleep well in Falkirk as there is a challenging 48 hours before us. First to Stirling and a fleet of venerable 'Midland Bluebird' Leyland Tiger buses is to take us to an unknown destination in the Grampian Mountains. The journey is mind-blowing, including the fearsome Devil's Elbow, one of the most difficult ascents in Scotland. However, our buses can tackle such obstacles though some need to stop for water at the designated point on the climb. We are dropped in the middle of nowhere armed with a map, compass, and handout, giving options for walking the 40-mile route in the subsequent 24 hours. Checkpoints have 'scores' assigned, so we have a choice; an easier and longer – or a harder and shorter but higher route and opt for the latter, which involves scaling three 'Munros'*. The team with the highest score arriving 30 minutes on either side of 24 hours is the winner. We don't win but are pleased to be awarded the *"best team from outside Scotland"* prize!

A stupid mistake, within ten minutes of starting, is to cross a fast-flowing river, water over our boots, to save time, instead of looking for stepping stones; it comes to haunt us when we get big blisters from our soaking socks!! Our route includes three peaks: An Socach, Beinn Iurthan Bheag, and Glas Tulaichen, each a 'Munro'; the first is scaled in the early evening, the second near midnight, and the third in the early hours of the morning. It is first light as we pause for rest on the Glas Tulaichen summit (3448 feet), where we witness a truly magical experience – it's not just the lovely view – it's **total silence**; a surreal feeling – no other people, no birds, no rushing water – and it's very beautiful! The remainder of the walk is downhill past Dalmunzie House stag hunting lodge to Spittal of Glenshee, where arrival is near to time; after 40 miles, getting on the return bus is agony as our blisters have swollen, and our host back at Falkirk insists that we all have a hot bath before providing a superb dinner.

---

* A 'Munro' is the name given to a mountain over 3000 feet.

Outdoors in West Yorkshire   ## A Mis- or Well-Spent Early Twenties

In early 1966, I am promoted to a job in the newly created computer-based train planning office in Leeds. It involves the input of data for computer programmers with prospects of rapid promotion to that grade or even higher for those with the aptitude which I discover I don't possess! However, I discover a very positive side to Leeds and West Yorkshire whereby masses of people head out to the Dales and Lakes every weekend: walking, climbing, caving, cycling (you name it, they do it); in contrast to South Wales where such activities are marginal. I stick at my boring job for eighteen months and sell my soul to the great outdoors. I take up running a scout troop and join the Otley rover scouts, and these, together with explorations by train over Northern England, uses up most weekends. If I needed a new awakening to outdoor life, this is it!

The Otley rovers, meeting weekly in the 'Red Lion', are very active with the outdoors, renting a barn loft in Blea Tarn Farm in Little Langdale. We tend to go every month or so and spend a lot of our time in the mountains around; fell walking, climbing and long sessions in the 'Old Dungeon Ghyll' pub. Most fell walking is on the Langdale Pikes and Bow Fell. I recall when we try to do England's highest peak, Scafell Pike, and are forced back by bad weather. It remains on my 'to do' list though, for health reasons, is now highly unlikely. I manage to make the summit of Bow Fell several times, though on one occasion, with scouts, retreat due to blizzard conditions.

Icy conditions on Bow Fell in Langdale.

The Yorkshire Dales is another frequent destination, and I manage the three main peaks, Penyghent, Whernside, and Ingleborough, on several occasions; the former is the most

Mike and his sons looking down from Ingleborough.

prominent and a personal favourite. On a March 1967 outing with local friend Mike and his two sons, we do Ingleborough, and I get a great view of the Settle to Carlisle railway, including photographing a steam-hauled freight train. Mike is a Yorkshireman through and through who describes his regular business trips over the Pennines to Oldham in Lancashire as *'missionary work!'*

I cycle a lot, and the bike comes in useful when I'm trying to find valuable locations for train photographs. I have a small flat in Bramhope, north of Leeds, almost above the two-mile-long Bramhope tunnel. I am there for several months before realising a steam train goes through the tunnel every Saturday lunchtime. It's the 12:50 Harrogate to King's Cross and is usually hauled by a 'Britannia' class locomotive. It's a steep ride down to see it at Arthington viaduct and appears to be even steeper coming back, which matters when the film runs out as the shot of the century appears! Undeterred, I go on several more Saturdays, but none is as good as the one that got away!

The elusive Harrogate to London train crossing the impressive viaduct at Arthington.

111

In March 1967, I go with the Otley rovers to Kingsdale Head near Ingleton, where we are manning a checkpoint on the celebrated 'Three Peaks Challenge,' a high-octane course of 24 miles which is expected to be done in under 12 hours, including scaling all three peaks. It's a real eye-opener from our tent, where we provide soup and hot drinks to the runners, most of whom don't stop as they pick them up on the go. Their fitness is something much to be admired!

Deep in the Yorkshire Dales near Ingleton, the Kingsdale Head checkpoint on the 'Three Peaks Challenge.'

Closer to home is beautiful Wharfedale, where the celebrated *'Ilkley Moor 'baht 'at'* is to be found. It's disappointing that it's not as exciting as much of the other landscapes in the dale, and I prefer upper Wharfedale for its range of dramatic scenery, the lovely villages including Burnsall and Kettlewell, and the fearsome 'Strid' river gorge.

1968?

Eighteen months soon goes as I resume my career with British Rail in earnest. I'm accepted as a management trainee and offered a choice of North Eastern or Western Region, opting for the latter based in the West of England.

Yorkshire is the catalyst that makes me into a true outdoors person, so I reckon sticking at a 'dead end' job is worth it after all. I miss 'gritty' West Yorkshire with memories of a soot-blackened Leeds Town Hall and lunchtime concerts by various brass bands. It is cleaned after I leave, but I reckon it looked better in black!

Mountaineering in Wester Ross

Beinn Eighe, Liathach, and the Torridons

A spectacular sunset over Loch Maree as we drop down into Kinlochewe on our arrival day.

Having had a quiet period of mountaineering since 1967, I am back with a vengeance in 1969 when I join two friends, David and Brian, on a mountain holiday in Wester Ross. We are all railwaymen. I travel up in David's car, and Brian joins us on site, having come up from Devon by train. Brian is a very keen mountaineer and has devised a full programme of peaks to be covered and, to soften the blow after hard days, books us into a guest house in the village of Kinlochewe, specialising in great breakfasts, dinners, and lunch packs. All we must do is walk and climb!

I meet David at Newport, and we travel up in the early afternoon in his 'MG-B.' In the days when such things could be done, he offers for me to drive part of the way to relieve him. I enjoy doing the 'ton' along parts of the M6 whilst David looks out for the traffic cops, and I do the same for him! We overnight at a B&B in the most idyllic village of Crawfordjohn, just off the A74 in Lanarkshire. My abiding memory is of a glorious sunset to the birdsong of Lapwings and Curlews. Refreshed, we set off on the next long road journey to Kinlochewe – not *'by Tummel and Loch Rannoch and Lochaber'* as the song goes – but a little further west via Tyndrum, Kinlochleven, and Fort William.

I don't recall the order of our mountains, but the weather is good enough for climbing on five of the six days (on a wet day, we travel the legendary lonely single track 'road to Applecross'). I'm amazed at the scale of the mountains in this part of Scotland. South is the main range dominated by Beinn Eighe (3314 feet), which we can see from our hotel and the first one that we tackle. The range consists of five peaks with 'Munro' status, and we scale at least three on the way to the main peak; the ups and downs are considerable, and we climb more than 5000 feet on this day.

The Beinn Eighe range from the main summit with *Liathach* in the background.

A scene of utter tranquillity and beauty. A distant view of Slioch from Loch Maree.

It's a tough start to the day, but the weather is good, sunny but not too warm, and we enjoy a great dinner on return to the hotel. We climb two mountains further west in the area known as Torridon; Liathach (3458 feet), which abuts the Beinn Eighe range, and above Loch Torridon is Bheinn Alligin (3232 feet). Both involve a lot of hard climbing though the latter, part of a smaller range, is a little easier.

On the north side of Loch Maree is the iconic Slioch (3215 feet), and its prominent rounded peak is visible from a great distance. Its position above but distant from the loch is quite stunning. There is no road access in the vicinity, so it's quite a long walk before we scale its peak. Further north and involving a lengthy car journey is An Teallach (3484 feet) and is a range with two peaks (the second is 3474 feet) and several other sub-peaks, all 'Munros,' so we 'bag' four more that day! The view from the top is quite stunning, and we can see across a large part of the Sutherland coasts and peaks (none of which are 'Munros'), including Stac Polaidh (2000'), which we also climb.

After probably one of my most strenuous weeks ever, we move on to the Lake District and include Helvellyn in our itinerary there, then home to South Wales.

The formidable Stac Polaidh (though it's not a 'Munro')

| Unfinished Business | Ben Nevis, at the Top of Britain |

The author looking tired but happy...

...and no wonder! Look at the view out to the coast and Hebrides

For all my mountaineering, I still haven't climbed all the highest mountains of the countries that make up mainland Britain. Ben Nevis, highest of all, is done in 1973, but it is over twenty years later, in 1997, when I finally tackle Snowdon, though Scafell Pike stays unchallenged by me despite a valiant attempt in 1967.

In October 1973, I travel to Scotland with Brian. He takes his car on the 'car-sleeper' train from Crewe to Inverness, followed by a ten-day motoring tour of the Highlands (Chapter 6). For the most part, the weather stays good, and we see some magnificent mountain scenery. Amongst those that we spot en route are the famous Five Sisters of Kintail, of which two are 'Munros.'

By the time we get to Fort William, the weather has improved a lot, and we decide to stay the night to tackle Ben Nevis *the* next day. Our accommodation is a modern budget motel which is, literally, cheap and nasty. After a lousy, so-called breakfast the next morning, we stock up on some decent picnic food and set out in bright sunshine for Glen Nevis. By the time we reach the car park, a thick fog has descended. Undeterred, we change into our boots and start the ascent. By the 1000-foot mark, it is brilliantly clear and sunny, but there is trouble. A lone walker following us says *"Does either of you own a Hillman Avenger?"* to which Brian replies, *"Yes."* The walker continues, *"Well, your headlights are on."* Panic, do we return to fix the car and add another thousand feet to our climb? We decide to proceed and hope there are people there on our return to help start the car.

The climb is steep with lots of scree in places, but in a couple of hours, we make the summit. Wow, what a sight! The air is clear, the sun is shining, the view is as good as it gets, and we can see as far as Skye and the Inner Hebrides; we're at the top of Britain!

The descent turns out to be a lot more difficult than the ascent due to the large amount of scree, and when we reach the parking lot, there are plenty of people to help start the car. We drive into Fort William and have a great dinner but stay somewhere nicer than the previous night!

Challenges in Wales

Brecon Beacons and Cader Idris

Pen-y-Fan (left) and Corn Du (right) on a better day than described in my ascent (below).

Whilst the greatest number of mountains I climb are in Scotland, I don't neglect my own country but don't manage to climb any peaks in North Wales until I tackle Snowdon itself in 1997. As mentioned elsewhere, my earliest climbs are in the Vale of Neath and the Brecon Beacons National Park, plus forays to the Mid Wales mountains of Plynlimon and Cader Idris.

My Pen-y-Fan climbs start with a few Boxing Day forays of the late 60s, but I manage to go up several times since then, most notably with Edward when we tackle the mountain from the Neuadd Reservoir to the south. When we start, it is raining, but this doesn't faze us; we are well equipped, even having a Primus stove and some packet soup to warm us up. We can't see far enough to realise there is snow, and lots of it, at the higher altitude; again, we take it in our stride. At the summit, in deep snow and windy conditions, I get the Primus fired up and realise we have no water; we are right idiots! No problem, we'll melt some snow and make water. It takes a long time to melt and then heat up, and by the time our soup is hot, we are in danger of 'exposure.' We drink it quickly and hasten back off the mountain.

Cader Idris from the south.

Some years later, with my friend Bob, a keen walker who I meet during my period in British Steel at Port Talbot, we do a midwinter climb on Fan Fawr on the far west edge of the Beacons. It is very cold, with deep snow and ice, but it's an exhilarating walk. I learn a lesson I should have known; don't drink and climb, as it makes the task much harder.

I consider *Cader Idris* to be one of the best peaks in Mid Wales, and I climb it three times, each from a different starting point and with difficulty. The west-facing ridge is almost sheer, and I guess is only doable by extreme rock climbing. On every visit, summit visibility is poor, and I'm unable to photograph the fantastic views out to sea, though I've seen this mountain many times from the train and interestingly once from a plane in sunny conditions and can vouch for its iconic beauty; it's a sight I can never tire of!

North Wales, the Ultimate Challenge — Yr Wyddfa Snowdon

Looking back from the path towards Llanberis, we get a panoramic view, including the little Snowdon Mountain Railway train.

Considering the number of times I've been to North Wales and seen the wonderful range of mountains in the National Park, its peaks have eluded me on many occasions until, in August 1997, I finally tackle the iconic Snowdon with friend and fellow scout leader Rob. We stay in Capel Curig with our wives, and they are off to Llandudno for shopping (they don't need any persuading!) while we prepare to climb from the Llanberis side, close to the railway. It is a long but not difficult trek, and the weather is sunny and hot, more of an impediment than the terrain. As we approach the summit, over the last few hundred feet, it gets distinctly cooler, and at the summit, there is a mist and a strong wind; and it feels more like March than August. We don't spend very long and make for the summit café and station. We take the train to Llanberis and get the last two tickets.

I've done the highest in Scotland and highest in Wales with Scafell Pike, highest in England, still unconquered, and it will have to stay that way; I've hung up my boots for good!

I finally make Snowdon with Rob *(Robert Jones)*.

A previous attempt to climb in Snowdonia is in 1973 when I join Brian for a long weekend in Penmaenmawr. The plan is to climb one of the Carneddau ranges, but the weather is unrelentingly bad, so they remain as unfinished business.

An English Miscellany — The Lakes, Kinder Scout, and Beacon Hill

In the early 1980s, I take up a job with British Rail in East Anglia. I like it, but there are no mountains, and I compensate by buying a house at Taverham near Norwich, which looks out on hills of 200 feet.

Through my association with the Scouts in Norwich, I often get out on coastal and country walks fine but not too challenging. There are two occasions when I go with the local venture scouts to the mountains. First to Edale in the Peak District and climb the famous Kinder Scout, the site of the first mass trespass of ramblers. The mountain is not difficult, but the route is long and the weather not kind; so bad in fact that the tent is flooded at night leaving me with a soggy sleeping bag, though luckily, I have a change of dry clothing.

The following year, I join the group on a weekend visit to the Lake District, to Langdale no less, an area I am familiar with from my sixties' Otley rover scout days. It's a very long way from Norwich, and setting out quite late on Friday afternoon we don't get to pitch our tents until the early hours of Saturday. The journey via a very flat Lincolnshire is interesting as we stop at Long Sutton for supper at a place named 'Agatha Crustie's'. On the wall is a notice board for the 'Fenland Mountain Rescue Team', practice every weekend on the tower of Ely Cathedral; I suppose in such flat country, you need that sort of humour.

To return to the Lake District, Saturday starts dry as we ascend Langdale Pikes but rapidly deteriorates to heavy rain by the end of the day. Sunday stays very wet all day, so there's little option but to stay and drink in the 'Old Dungeon Ghyll' for the rest of the day! By Monday morning, our field is a river, and we discover the tents, pitched in darkness, are on the only high ground and consequently not flooded! I need to paddle through running water to get to the land rover where my office suit is hanging, and I arrange to be dropped at Oxenholme to travel south to attend a course at Watford. As I wait for my train, the 'Advanced Passenger Train', on test, rushes through on reverse curves, lurching violently from side to side (the inside stays level, that's the theory!), and I bet none of the waiting passengers would travel on it after that. No worries, it never comes into service and ends up in a railway museum!

Finally, and with tongue firmly in cheek, I arrange a venture scout/ranger guide expedition to scale Norfolk's highest peak, 10,000 centimetres (330 feet) Beacon Hill above Sheringham. Our party wades out of the sea at Sheringham, tackles the peak by the steep 'north face,' arriving on the summit at midnight; our antics are being fully trailed on local Radio Norfolk, and we attract much interest and admiration for tackling such a formidable peak. Little do they know it's me taking an aside at the flatness of the landscape, and I just couldn't have left the county without having scaled its highest point!

Beacon Hill, Sheringham (note the north face, ahead, left! *(hillexplorer.com)*.

In 1962, a train from Brecon to Moat Lane Junction leaving Rhayader station, a most picturesque location.

I am very fortunate that for my working life and beyond, I have the advantage of reduced rate or free train travel in the UK, and the only impediment in Wales is the relative difficulty of getting to many parts of the country by train after the 'Beeching' closures take effect. The period from the late 60s to 2005 is the worst as frequencies and connections are sub-optimal. Thereafter, great improvements as a much-improved service timetable with better connections make train travel much easier.

In late 1982, I am promoted back to Wales from East Anglia to manage passenger services in South and West Wales, and in 1988, my area is expanded to cover the whole of Wales. Thus, I have one of the most attractive railway networks anywhere in Europe with responsibilities for business planning and marketing. Along with the beautiful rural and coastal scenery come huge challenges as these railways don't make any money. Indeed, they lose money in varying degrees, and the common objective is to save costs and improve incomes. This is the subject of another book, I guess!

For now, it's good to reflect that I had stewardship of these lines operating as they do in the most scenically stunning locations, and for that, I am thankful for almost twelve years of direct involvement. This has helped me to select what is my choice of Wales's finest railway journeys, namely:

- The Cambrian Coast Line
- The Central Wales (now Heart of Wales) Line
- The Mid Wales Line

For these, I attempt to paint a picture of what I find attractive, the people I meet, the incidents, and their ups and downs. The Mid Wales line doesn't outlive 1962, and thus my narrative is of reminiscences.

The Cambrian Coast Line | Aberystwyth to Pwllheli

The best railway view in the UK, the *Cambrian Coast Express* crossing Barmouth viaduct,
Cader Idris in background.

he said Scotland was best!

From my very first magical journey along the Cambrian Coast in 1953, it has become my favourite line in the UK and even beyond. How can one fail to be attracted by a railway traversing wonderful scenery expressed through its coastal views and backdrop of mountains. Amplified by the sheer variety of steam train operations and even including developments with more modern traction up to the present, it is good to see this railway still in such good health with a scenic backdrop to die for.

On my 1953 visit, most of the trains are in the hands of ex-GWR locomotives, necessarily small types due to the restrictive route availability. Largest are the handsome 'Manor' class, usually entrusted with longer trains, and the 'Cambrian Coast Express.' At that time, there are a few small BR Standard locomotives and ex-Cambrian Railways small tender locomotives (one new Standard replaces one old Cambrian). By the time of my 1962 visit, the small tank engines are replaced by BR Standard types ousting most of the ex-GWR locomotives. Steam is set to disappear and, by 1966, remains mainly on summer Saturdays. By that time, it is just standard Class 4 types and English Electric class 37 diesels, all other trains being operated by first generation diesel railcars.

A busy period at Dovey Junction with a train to Pwllheli (left) connecting with a train from Aberystwyth (right).

The first generation railcar era; view from the train approaching Morfa Mawddach.

A short section at the north end between Afon Wen and Pwllheli also hosts ex-LMS locomotives that work down from Bangor and Caernarfon. These trains never make it to the diesel age as the 'Beeching' cuts intervene, and the line from Caernarfon is closed.

The Cambrian system has essentially four divisions; the main line from Shrewsbury to Aberystwyth, the Coast line from Machynlleth to Pwllheli, the Ruabon-Barmouth line, and the ex-LMS line from Caernarfon to Afon Wen (Porthmadog and Pwllheli). Two named trains run year-round, the 'Cambrian Coast Express' from London Paddington to Aberystwyth and Pwllheli, dividing at Machynlleth, and 'the Welshman' from London Euston to Porthmadog and Pwllheli, dividing at Afon Wen. Other trains are local with frequent stops and at roughly two-hourly intervals. In both 1962 and 1963, Hugh and I spend several days on the Cambrian system and notice the gradual change of steam traction, the most notable being the advent of the Standard locomotives displaced from other routes by electrification, many in a run-down condition. In 1966, Robert and I see firsthand the consequential operating problems on our visit to Machynlleth (Chapter 3). My next visit to the Cambrian is in the early 1980s when I'm there for the grand extension of the 'Ffestiniog Railway' through to Blaenau Ffestiniog, and I return to Shrewsbury on a diesel railcar struggling with the schedule as only one of its two cars is powered. This is rectified in 1985 with the introduction of new Class 150/1 'Sprinters.' When my role expands to take in all of Wales's services in January 1988, I inherit a 'Cambrian,' which is 'all-Sprinter' operation, and 'Radio Electronic Token Signalling' (RETB), the first of its type in Britain.

Penultimate traction type is the Class 156 Sprinter seen here crossing Barmouth viaduct.

The 1986 excursion returning to London Euston from Barmouth.

In 1985, there is a crisis as the Barmouth viaduct is closed to locomotives, its timbers attacked by the 'teredo worm,' but at least remedial work is done. By April 1986, it's complete, and I am invited to witness the special re-opening train from London Euston with two EE Class 37 diesels and a rake of newly liveried intercity coaches, a great sight! A special is also run from Barmouth to Pwllheli, and it's my first cab ride on a Sprinter.

From early 1988 to 1991, now with responsibility for the Cambrian lines, I can't believe my luck inheriting this iconic railway. It is not without problems, as 'RETB' and new rolling stock beds in, but the basics are sound, and improvements are made to the timetable to the Midlands by extending trains beyond Wolverhampton to Birmingham, and the '150' type is replaced with an improved version. In 1990, the 'Cambrian Coast Express' through train to London is withdrawn and is replaced by a 'Sprinter' to Birmingham. The next and final rolling stock change is made in 1994 with the allocation of 'Express' Class 158 railcars, together with dramatic line speed improvements of up to 80 mph between Shrewsbury and Machynlleth.

There are two successful attempts to return steam operation on the Coast Line; first in 1987 when 7819 'Hinton Manor' does a few trips out of Machynlleth; and an annual programme commences in 2005 for the next six years, the principal power being a BR Standard Class 4 with an ex-LMS 'Black 5' in the penultimate year of operation. I ride it on three occasions, some very nostalgic trips. The later introduction of sophisticated 'ETCS' signalling using the 'Cambrian' Lines as a testbed puts a stop to steam operation though there is some hope that a technical 'fix' can be found that will enable steam to resume before too long.

A Class 158 'Express' railcar seen here at Llangelynin, north of Tywyn.

The Central Wales Line — Swansea to Shrewsbury

On a lovely July evening in 1963, the Swansea to York Mail approaching Mumbles Road with Swansea Bay in the background.

The Central Wales Line (now known as the 'Heart of Wales Line) is close to my heart. Running originally from Swansea Victoria station to Shrewsbury, the section from Swansea to Pontarddulais closed in 1964. My first connection is in the mid-1950s when attending county cricket matches at St Helen's ground, conveniently opposite Swansea Bay station. I am always more interested in observing the railway scene and the adjacent 'Mumbles Train' than watching cricket. The local trains to Pontarddulais are hauled by ex-LNWR 'Coal Tanks,' replaced around 1959 by ex-LMS 'Jinties' and finally by ex-GWR 'Pannier Tanks'. The Shrewsbury trains are the preserve of a small fleet of ex-LMS 'Black Fives,' all based at Shrewsbury, right to the end of steam operation. In the late 1950s, Standard Class 4 locomotives are trialled – unsuccessfully – and in the early 60s, the depot at Shrewsbury gets a small allocation of Standard class 5's. In 1963, a few displaced Standard tank engines are allocated to Swansea East Dock depot and work some Shrewsbury trains. The story doesn't end there, as in 1964, Shrewsbury gets some cascaded ex-LMS 'Jubilee' class, but though they are more powerful, their large driving wheels make them less suited to this heavily graded line.

The final York Mail at Pontarddulais in June 1964.

In June 1964, the last train from Swansea Victoria, the 1830 hrs to York, is hauled by 'Black Five' 45406. From then, trains run between Llanelli and Shrewsbury four times a day with Swindon-built diesel railcars. The line survives a few closure proposals as it *"passes through four marginal constituencies"* and is still operating to the present day. The railcars are replaced by 'Metro-Cammell's in the 1970s, 'Derby Lightweight's in 1986; and finally, by single car 'Sprinters' in 1993.

In March 1963, Britain is in the grip of a long-term freeze that lasts more than two months. I am working in Swansea District Office, and on the first week of heavy snow, I am redeployed on night shifts to the Control Office as a record keeper. Motive power is disrupted, and unusual sightings include a '2251' class (Knighton banker) on a passenger train as well as an ex-LMS 'Crab,' most unusual. Best is when the southbound York-Swansea Mail is held at Llandovery as the gates are frozen. I'm told not to record that the driver is instructed to use his locomotive to open them!

For over sixty years, I retain an association with this line and can recount many interesting experiences, first in 1959 when I make use of a week-long 'holiday runabout ticket' for just 19/6 (c.£1 new money), and do three return journeys. Each time, I take the 07:45 Swansea Victoria to Shrewsbury; on the first day, a Saturday, it has 8 coaches double-headed by two ex-LMS freight locomotives, and the train is through to Manchester. The following week it's an ex-LMS 'Fowler' tank, then a 'Black Five', so there's plenty of variety. From Shrewsbury, I go on to Crewe, Chester, and Wrexham on consecutive days.

In 1963, I am transferred to work at the newly opened Landore Diesel Depot and soon find it provides the drivers for the Central Wales trains. The two daily turns both of 11 hours 30 mins, are much sought after for overtime and mileage payments. I get friendly with drivers and, on my rest days, arrange rides on the footplate. The best is in November 1963 when I go through to Shrewsbury and back; the driver and fireman make for an entertaining team. Driver Gordon is a car enthusiast, has an 'Armstrong Siddeley', and I join him in Landore; he wears a suit, drives to Victoria station, and changes into overalls. As we board our BR Standard Class 5, he promises an entertaining ride and he's not kidding! Near Builth, he stops between stations, the fireman jumps down and tosses apples from a nearby orchard, and we get on our way. Shrewsbury is reached without further incident. We take an hour's break and pick up the 14:40 return with another BR Standard Class 5 feeling and looking very rough. It steams poorly on the climb to Church Stretton; on to Craven Arms at speed, there's a bad knocking sound which Gordon takes in his stride. It's a struggle uphill to Llangynllo, but then we gain speed on to Llandrindod. It is after Builth Road that the fun starts; at Cilmeri, with the A483 alongside, a sports car driver signals he wants a race! Gordon is supercharged, *"okay, you b......d, I'll give you a race,"* opens the regulator wide, and we accelerate noisily, but the road is sinuous, and we get ahead. A mile on, climbing out of Garth, we run short of steam and stop for some time for the fire to be rebuilt. By now, we are all filthy from the smoke, so at Llandeilo, Gordon goes into the train for a wash. The fireman takes control and leaves me to do the firing as far as Pantyffynnon. On arrival at Swansea, tired and filthy, I draw odd looks from passengers on the bus back to Neath!

It's deep winter and very cold as a diesel railcar climbs the last mile
from Cynghordy to the Sugar Loaf tunnel in December 1990.

'Jubilee' 45660 *Rooke* at Llandovery in January 1964.

Other footplate trips haven't been so lively, but there's one left to mention. A 'Jubilee' is on the 09:45 from Swansea in January 1964 and Robert and I are invited to fire on different sections of the trip to Llandovery.

Twenty years on, I'm the 'guv'nor'; no more messing about. As Passenger Manager, I am responsible for all train services in the Valleys, South and West Wales, including Central Wales. For the next eight years, with this line having the lowest income, I am stretched to deal with management matters in my own time, as there are so many other issues higher up the chain. The local user group 'HoWLTA' (which still exists) is ever helpful and provides a Santa Claus in the guards' van of the train from Llandovery pre-Christmas 1984 and 1985. There's a good spirit, and a lot gets done, but much more needs to be done to cut costs and improve income. Over the next few years, all signal boxes except Pantyffynnon and Craven Arms are closed, and 'electric train token,' a safe system for single lines dating back 100 years, is implemented. This transfers duties from the signalmen to drivers, using cabins placed on platforms; some level crossings become semi-automated, the passing loop at Llandrindod Wells is transferred from north of the station back into the station, and finally, a new loop is provided at Knighton cutting out a very long single line section; all are done with at least 75% of public money.

There is a tragedy as well; in October 1987, a storm flood washes away the foundations of the bridge piers at Glanrhyd, south of Llandovery, resulting in the train hitting the water with the loss of four lives; this bridge is replaced nine months later with a fine lattice girder structure.

A new service is introduced, adding one through train each way to the previous four. The fleet of diesel railcars is replaced with a more reliable type, and the revenue/cost ratio improves greatly. In 1989, with a grant from the 'Sports Council for Wales' topped with BR money, a

Sunday 'Recreation Rambler' train is introduced, becomes a great success, and helps establish regular Sunday services. Over these years, I make many trips along the line and take delight in seeing these improvements come to fruition.

Families wait to board the 'Recreation Rambler' at Pantyffynnon in July 1989

Cynghordy viaduct in 1963 with a Shrewsbury-bound train.

In 1982, with track conditions poor, the Regional Civil Engineer imposes a ban on locomotive haulage, which knocks out special trains until the area engineer gets it lifted four years later with a limit of one train per week, enough to get some regular charter trains – steam and diesel hauled – on the line every year since.

In 1993 the newly created 'Regional Railways' is in cost-cutting mode and pares Central Wales services down to four each way, a situation pertaining to the present time. There is an encouraging announcement from new owners Transport for Wales that the fifth train will resume in late 2022, almost 40 years on! I retain a close association with the Line as a director of the Heart of Wales Development Company which should keep me active for some time!

A 'Sprinter' in 'Transport for Wales' livery near Cynghordy *(Stephen Miles)*.

Through all these years, what fascinates me is the sheer variety that typifies not only the trains but also the terrain. Taking the pre-1964 situation, starting with a pleasant seaside run alongside Swansea Bay, followed by a steep climb to Gowerton, the 20 miles of mining and industrial landscape before the bucolic Towy Valley between Llandeilo and Llandovery. Then an abrupt change with the long climb to Sugar Loaf summit, crossing the first of two very graceful viaducts on the line at Cynghordy, followed by the long and narrow tunnel under Sugar Loaf Mountain. Next is the iconic Spa of Llanwrtyd, the smallest town in Britain, and much easier terrain along the Irfon Valley to Builth Road, followed by a climb out of the valley to Llandrindod Wells, the principal settlement along the route. The scenery changes to a stretch of open moorland before dropping down steeply to Knighton, crossing the second notable viaduct at Knucklas. In this section is the delightful Dolau station, winner of floral displays for more years than I can remember and giving impetus for similar adornment all along the line. Knighton is a lovely town situated on the famous 'Offa's Dyke'; it's a curiosity that although the town is in Powys, Wales, its station is in Shropshire, England; a fact that comes to light when European grant funding towards the new station loop is held up until it's established to be for the benefit of a Welsh town! From here on, the railway is in England and the countryside is open and very attractive. The line proper ends at Craven Arms, where trains join the Marches Line through to Shrewsbury.

The Mid Wales Lines

Brecon to Moat Lane Junction

The 16:05 Hereford to Brecon waits patiently for the late running 17:05 from Brecon at Talgarth. That has waited at Talyllyn Junction for the late running 15:00 from Newport, itself having waited for a late running 11:55 from Paddington. Complicated?

This railway closed almost sixty years ago and must be the finest of the inland routes in Wales. It links with the Cambrian main line five miles west of Newtown at remote Moat Lane Junction, quite a romantic name for a station in the middle of nowhere. From here on, it runs almost due south to Brecon through some significant towns: Llanidloes, Rhayader, Builth Wells, and Talgarth. It has an interchange with the Central Wales line at Builth Road. Soon after is Three Cocks Junction, where the line from Hereford joins, then Talyllyn Junction, where the line south to Newport leaves. From Brecon, there is a link south to Neath, which closes two months before the rest. Brecon, though not a junction station, is the most important hub on the network. This substantial town loses all its railways at a stroke in a similar fashion to the county town of Monmouth some years earlier. During the time that I'm able to enjoy the use of the line, its attraction can hardly be variety in locomotives as all trains are hauled by the handsome ex-LMS 'Ivatt' Class 2's, necessary due to weight restrictions on the line.

They follow similarly lightweight ex-GWR 'Dean Goods' or ex-Cambrian Railways locomotives, both types with tenders having the ability to carry enough coal for long journeys is essential.

Three Cocks Junction, three-way connections to Builth Road (left), Brecon (centre), and Hereford (right).

Brecon is the hub of this system of four lines; its four platforms are only all in use once a day around 18:00.

The post-1958 timetable is a masterly attempt to link with the many connecting services as a rationalisation at the time cuts out duplicate trains between Brecon and Three Cocks. This, along with superb scenery, makes the route operationally and aesthetically interesting. The short three-mile hop from Brecon to Talyllyn Junction is quite heavily graded, but the line settles down to an even grade thereon to Three Cocks Junction through the superb pastoral countryside. Here, the Hereford line leaves, after which the Mid Wales line runs along the well wooded banks of the River Wye to Builth Wells and on to Rhayader. This is, in my view, by far the most scenic part of the route. After Rhayader, it climbs steeply out from the Wye Valley to the summit at Pantydwr, followed by an equally steep drop through Tylwch to Llanidloes. The large station building here, one time headquarters of the Cambrian Railway, nowadays stands incongruously over the town's by-pass. Llanidloes is the principal station on the line after Brecon, and there are four local trains between here and Moat Lane each day. South of here, the track bed of the proposed (though never completed) 'Manchester & Milford Railway' came in. A little known, more recent fact is that Llanidloes was to become a railhead in the 1970s for the supply of materials for building a super-size Elan Valley Reservoir with a 3/4-mile-wide dam which never gets beyond the drawing board. The line goes through Llandinam (birthplace of David Davies, promoter of both the 'Cambrian Railway' and the failed M&M) and then along the level Clywedog valley, a tributary of the river Severn, to reach the impressive-looking Moat Lane Junction. Passengers wouldn't die of thirst on the Mid Wales line as all junctions include a pub on the station platform!

The Mid Wales Line passes through a variety of landscapes; here at Llangorse Lake, it is very pastoral.

A busy scene at Talyllyn Junction where the train from Newport has arrived (left)
and the Moat Lane train waits (right).

A few words on the two interesting lines that leave the Mid Wales Line. First, that to Newport, which passes over part of the Brecon Beacons and through the famous Torpantau tunnel, topping a gruelling seven-mile grade at 1 in 39. The intermediate station of Pentir Rhiw was connected by footpath to the nearest road; its signal box achieved TV fame in the early 1960s with the *'Davy Jones' Locker'* serial.

From Talyllyn Junction, the line follows the bucolic Usk Valley to Talybont before beginning the long severe climb to Torpantau, dropping past the Taff Fechan Reservoir to Pontsticill Junction where a branch to Merthyr Tydfil trails off right, then through Pant (restored as narrow-gauge *Brecon Mountain Railway*) and Dowlais, through a fascinating post-industrial landscape and down the valley to Bargoed. From here, it crosses a few other valley lines, eventually emerging east of Caerphilly and to Newport via Bassaleg Junction. A route of great interest and variety.

The afternoon Hereford to Brecon pauses at Hay on Wye;
note the Midland-style running board and signal box.

The Hereford line diverges east at Three Cocks and is a most attractive country route. The soil hereabouts is a rich red colour, and the villages served are delightful. The main station on the route is Hay-on-Wye, famous these days as one of the World's 'Book Towns' hosting an annual literary festival; would that it still had a train link! Originally conceived by the Midland Railway and included the line from Brecon to Swansea, its purpose was to tap anthracite coal traffic destined for the Midlands.

Finally, a brief mention of the Brecon to Neath railway, an oddity caused by the Midland Railways' withdrawal from Swansea. When I first know it, there are three daily trains on weekdays, but in 1958, it is reduced to one per day with a Saturday extra; that allows me to get to Hereford or Rhayader and back before the evening train from Brecon.

A train from Kyle of Lochalsh to Inverness approaching Achnasheen.

Scotland is an outstanding country in terms of its scenery, history, and culture. Many very fine and world-class train journeys remain to the present day. Some scenic routes are lost forever, notably the Port Road from Dumfries to Stranraer, Callander & Oban between Dunblane and Crianlarich, and the rail network in the Borders, including the remains of the Waverley route south of Tweedbank (though there are hopes of an eventual restoration of this one).

My journeys include some of the scenic gems and the Glasgow to Aberdeen route in steam and early diesel days.

- The West Highland Line
- The Kyle and Far North Lines
- The Glasgow to Aberdeen Line

Glenfinnan, of 'Bonnie Prince Charlie' fame, midway between Mallaig and Fort William.

The West Highland Line — Glasgow to Oban and Mallaig

The wild and remarkable Rannoch Moor can be enjoyed in full only from the train.

This remarkable route hardly needs an introduction and has featured on so many television programmes of late. For me, over thirty-two years, it becomes very familiar, and I make the journeys over all or part of the route on no fewer than ten occasions.

My first introduction is at Mallaig in 1965, having arrived from Kyle of Lochalsh, two ferries and a bus, as part of a grand tour of Scotland with Robert. We travel on to Fort William, stay two nights and continue to Glasgow. It makes an instant impression as it is so spectacular, and I vow I must come back. That day comes three years later when I replicate the trip though, without a stay in Fort William. I'm back again in 1970 with an overnight stop at remote Corrour (Chapter 6).

It's 1976 before I reach Oban, a line with very different – though also spectacular – scenery, and 1984 before I am in the West Highlands again for my only trip on the steam train between Fort William and Mallaig as well as a one-way trip from Oban to Glasgow. Between 1987 and 1997, I make more trips to Mallaig and Fort William and a return trip between Glasgow and

Tulloch, out with diesel and back with steam; more on this later. Four of these are made in winter as part of itineraries ending up in Edinburgh for rugby, some by through sleeping car train from London Euston.

Glasgow train ready to leave Oban in summer 1976.

Ben Nevis completely dominates the town of Fort William

Motive power for these trains changes several times though is various type 2 diesels, mostly 'BRCW' but with 'North British' types appearing in 1968 only to revert later, due to unreliability issues. By the 80s, motive power throughout the Highlands is the ubiquitous English Electric class 37 diesel locomotive. By the time of my final trip in 1997, return from Fort William is in a 'Sprinter,' which by this time is the staple for all West Highland trains except the 'Sleeper.'

My steam experiences are nine years apart. 1984 is the first year of what is to become a very successful programme of steam trains between Fort William and Mallaig though I travel only on the outward journey, returning by service train. In 1993, I am invited to have a free trip on a special train organised by 'SLOA' from Birmingham to Fort William in recognition of my facilitation of that company's West Wales steam train programme earlier in the year. It is booked for a Class 37 diesel from Edinburgh, but at Craigendoran, the train crew relief hasn't turned up; our diesel returns to Glasgow and changing crews causes a two-hour delay. It terminates at Tulloch, where the steam locomotive arrives from Fort William to take us back to Glasgow!

The West Highland line is a joy to travel on from the start at Craigendoran through to Mallaig and the spur to Oban. It is heavily graded over much of its length as it passes through amazing mountain and moorland scenery. A through 'Sleeper' from London Euston runs throughout my travels. The Oban branch leaves at Crianlarich for a spectacular run through the Pass of Brander; and the main line continues over wild Rannoch Moor to Fort William, in the shadow of Ben Nevis. From here to Mallaig is the best part, with spectacular views of the mountains, lochs, and the wonderful sight of the Isle of Skye across the water from Morar.

The steam train starts as the 'West Highlander' in its first year, 1984, and is an immediate success. As marketing is ramped up in subsequent years, its name is changed to the far more exciting 'Jacobite,' and a second daily round trip is added in high season. Its popularity is undiminished, and it is regularly fully booked. The power of steam and scenery!

The Skye and Far North Lines	Inverness to Kyle of Lochalsh, Wick and Thurso

The western part of the line to Kyle of Lochalsh runs alongside the stunning Loch Carron.

The city of Inverness is known as the capital of the Highlands. It's also the terminus for the remarkable Highland main line from Glasgow and Edinburgh and a cross-country route from Aberdeen. Here is where two spectacular lines start, and both have unique but different features that put them in the top bracket of scenic railways. First is the 82-mile line to Kyle of Lochalsh, and the second, is the amazing 161-mile line to Wick and Thurso, the most northerly stations in Britain.

I travel several times on both lines, which share a common route for the first 19 miles to Dingwall, where the Kyle line veers off in a westerly direction, and the Far North line goes, well, north! Both are threatened with closure in the 'Beeching' years but survive due to their status as important lifelines for the communities they serve.

Locomotive haulage has been the rule during the whole period of my journeys, though since then, diesel multiple unit operation has become the norm.

As observed, the two lines have different scenic characteristics; the Kyle line goes through a mountainous country with the last 20 miles along incredibly beautiful Loch Carron. There are no towns on the route, and the settlements served are very small. At Achnasheen, 60 miles from Inverness, two post bus routes connect to west coast villages, and at Kyle of Lochalsh, there is a car ferry to Kyleakin on Skye and a packet boat to Stornoway on Lewis. Since my last trip, though, everything has changed. Skye is connected to the mainland by a bridge, and the Stornoway route is now a car ferry from Ullapool. The old order is over, and with it, I guess, some of the charm.

At Kyleakin on Skye, the car ferry arrives from Kyle of Lochalsh and is met by a MacBrayne's bus to Armadale.

A northbound train to Wick entering the wild and beautiful 'flow country' north of Helmsdale in 1963.

The Far North line is very different and most unusual in that it must make two separate diversions away from the coast, adding 40 miles to the more direct journey by road. That said, it is a route of great scenic variety with long, wild, coastal sections and brief forays into mountains and moorland. North from Dingwall to the Dornoch Forth is a gentler coast, and the Black Isle is to the east. Tain and Invergordon are modest towns but the largest, Dornoch, is off the railway though it was once served by a short branch from The Mound. The railway swings west, north, then east through the village of Lairg, where no fewer than three postbus routes connect to Tongue, Durness, and Lochinver. The train regains the coast again at Golspie and from here north is much wilder and very beautiful with long sandy beaches. At Brora, most trains cross, and from Helmsdale, the line again swings to the north-west and describes a large arc through the fascinating 'flow country,' a massive peat bog, much of which is under threat of forest planting. The train arrives at remote Georgemas Junction, which is where the Thurso branch and its shuttle goes off north while the main train travels 14 miles on to the terminus at Wick, 161 miles from Inverness. Some journey!

View from Tain station over the Dornoch Firth; the line arcs inland through Lairg and is 25 miles longer than the road distance.

Since my last journey, big changes have been made, and there has been rationalisation, Thurso is served direct 'in and out,' doubling back to continue to Wick, adding to the overall journey. The service is now operated by 'Super Sprinter' diesel multiple units.

Both lines, particularly to Kyle, are frequented by charter trains, some very luxurious 'grand tours' of Scotland and sometimes of Great Britain. The regular services, still at the traditional low frequencies, are the subject of studies that could see better-rolling stock running more frequently and faster.

Glasgow to Aberdeen in 3 hours

A Mid-1960's Regular Steam Triumph

The 'Granite City' hauled by 60019 *Bittern* leaving Perth for Glasgow in the early evening.

The traditional route to Aberdeen north of Perth has been through Strathmore via Forfar and Glamis. This is a very fast line but doesn't serve many communities of any size and is near the longer route serving the large city of Dundee. It's not surprising that it succumbs to closure and trains are diverted via Dundee, but before this happens, the Scottish Region decides to accelerate four named trains with a city-to-city headline timing of three hours for the 153-mile journey with five stops (with some mile-a-minute timings between stops). This fits nicely with the cascade of 'A4 Pacifics', which have a long-deserved reputation for speed ('Mallard' was the World's fastest steam locomotive – 126 mph in 1938), from the East Coast Main Line and six of these are allocated to Glasgow's Eastfield depot for this purpose.

In April 1965, Robert and I start a week's Scottish holiday with our first trip to Stranraer, returning to Carlisle where we take a Euston-Perth express hauled by 'Britannia' *Hereward the Wake* and alight at Stirling. That afternoon, we take the 'St Mungo' through from Stirling

chairman of LNER

to Aberdeen, hauled by A4 *Sir Ralph Wedgewood*. Then we have our first high-speed run, particularly between Stanley Junction, north of Perth, and Kinnaber Junction near Montrose with its long straight sections of track; very exhilarating!

We spend the night in Aberdeen and are up early for the early morning 'Bon Accord,' hauled again by *Sir Ralph Wedgewood,* which we take as far as Stonehaven. We return to Aberdeen and travel a short way on the Deeside line and back in time for the mid-day 'St Mungo,' hauled by A4 *William Whitelaw*. The journey is through to Gleneagles, and we are again to enjoy a spirited performance through Strathmore.

chairman of LNER

For the second day running, we pick up the Euston-Perth train, this time at Gleneagles, again hauled by *Hereward the Wake*! We alight at Perth and wait for the 'Bon Accord,' which arrives behind a 'Black Five,' substituting for an A4. We are only going as far as Forfar, so it will be interesting to see if it gets up a good turn of speed for the 30-mile journey with one stop at Coupar Angus. It doesn't disappoint, and we are thrilled as it manages to keep time on its tight schedule.

Substituting for an A4, 'Black Five' 44794 passing Gleneagles with the southbound 'Saint Mungo'.

We stay the night in Forfar and leave early on the next day's 'Bon Accord,' which is hauled by its booked A4, this time, it's *Bittern*. We take this as far as Perth, where we bid farewell to our high-speed steam trains and prepare to head north to Inverness and beyond. A few days later, Robert and I part company as I must be back at work, and he decides to stay for a few more days' travel behind the A4s. I return via Edinburgh and then the 'Waverley' route to Carlisle (some four years before it closes throughout).

The era of the A4s on the three-hour Aberdeen trains comes to an end in the summer of 1966, with the final one withdrawn from service in September of that year. The Strathmore route is closed, and Glasgow-Aberdeen trains are routed via Dundee Tay Bridge. It has been an exhilarating experience to travel behind some of the Worlds' fastest steam locomotives for the last time. It's the end of an era and the start of a very different one.

The attractive harbour at the popular fishing port of Mevagissey.

Outside of my native South Wales, one part of England is to dominate my life in the 1950s. The West Country is where most of our family holidays are taken; Torquay in 1951 and 1957, Minehead in 1952, Newquay in 1954, Exmouth in 1955, and a scout camp to Penzance in 1956. I become very knowledgeable about the southwest and in particular its railways. I get my first train spotting book in 1952 and spent a whole Saturday in Taunton collecting numbers on a busy day of holiday expresses.

I am destined to spend much more time in the region in the late 1960s when my management training base is at Bristol in the West of England Division of British Rail. I travel over virtually all extant lines in this time, including the freight-only branch, to Fowey working on a project involving China Clay traffic. I get up close to the ex-Southern route from London Waterloo to Exeter in another project taking three months in late 1968. Though I return to South Wales for my post-training and subsequent jobs for the next ten years, my friend and colleague Paul is allocated a job in the West Country which he manages to hold for ten years, and I make frequent trips to stay with him discovering many new places off the beaten track.

Since then, I return many times, sometimes on day trips and occasionally on short breaks and holidays, the last being to Falmouth in 2019. In the remainder of this chapter, I will take my reader over some of my favourite train trips and a look at the splendid coast and countryside of this magnificent area.

Fascinating Train Journeys | Tiverton and Its Junction to Hemyock

Bucolic and busy. Locomotive 1442 shunts oil and milk tank cars at Hemyock.

A great place to start is in deepest Devon, where up to the early 1960s are to be found charming branch lines, and the most interesting must be the deep rural line between Tiverton Junction to sleepy Hemyock, nestled in the Blackdown Hills south of Taunton. Its advertised passenger service survives on the back of milk and freight traffic from Hemyock, and an ancient single carriage is attached to the rear of milk tanks, oil tanks, and grain wagons for a 7.5-mile journey taking around 45 minutes. I am the sole passenger both ways on what is probably the last true 'mixed' train in Britain.

On the journey, it stops to shunt at Uffculme (grain and fertiliser) and, on arrival at Hemyock, detaches empty milk tanks, shunts into the dairy sidings, then picks up loaded ones. There are empty oil tanks that conveyed fuel for the dairies returning to Avonmouth. The passenger carriage is shunted into the platform and takes up the rear for the return journey. Fascinating!

Time is made up on return by not shunting en route. At Tiverton Junction, I spot a westbound freight going through with an ex-GWR large freight locomotive. On the far platform, an auto train is waiting with the 'Tivvy Bumper' shuttle to Tiverton Town. Arrival there is at school homegoing time, and east- and west-bound Exe Valley trains are also there; all three leave simultaneously, each with a good complement of school children. The Hemyock line closes soon after, followed a year later by the Tiverton Junction and the Exe Valley line. The junction station also closes and, years later, is to be replaced by a brand-new Tiverton Parkway.

for passengers. Milk traffic lasted until c. 1970?

School trains rush hour at Tiverton Town station.

Fascinating Train Journeys 2 | The Southern Railways's 'withered arm'

Exeter St David's: a train to Ilfracombe conveys a through carriage from Waterloo;
its locomotive is a 'Bulleid' light pacific.

The *'withered arm'* refers to the network of ex-Southern Railway lines west of Exeter, most of which are now gone forever (or perhaps not*). Many see it as a conspiracy as the Western takes over from the Southern Region and finds these routes a distraction. Exeter-Barnstaple and Plymouth-Gunnislake are to remain, and what joy, the line to Okehampton reopens to passengers* in November 2021!

My first contact with these lines is brief. In 1952, when I travel between Ilfracombe and Barnstaple; and in 1954, between Padstow and Wadebridge. In 1962, I make a concerted effort to travel on all the lines and, over three days, cover the main line to Plymouth via Okehampton, the Padstow and Bude branches, and the 'unusual' line from Halwill Junction to Torrington. The following year, I return to Devon to complete the network; the Bere Alston to Callington branch and the ex-Southern branch lines in East Devon (except, to my great regret, not to Seaton and Lyme Regis).

I did

The Southern Railway/Region runs through carriages to all the north coastal destinations year-round on the famous 'Atlantic Coast Express' with portions for Exmouth, Sidmouth, Ilfracombe, Torrington, Bude, Padstow, and Plymouth. On Saturdays, each coastal terminus has its own through train from London Waterloo.

An express from Waterloo arrives at Exeter Central with a 'Merchant Navy' *locomotive* to be replaced by a smaller, lighter one for the journey west.

Bude: An afternoon train to Halwill Junction (where it will join up with a Padstow portion) for the journey to Exeter Central.

I suppose that my first link with the ex-Southern lines from Exeter is seeing the procession of trains to and from the Atlantic coast mixing with an even greater one of Western Region trains serving the south Devon and Cornwall resorts on a summer Saturday in July 1957. It's as close as I get to a railway 'heaven' – if such exists – with express trains hauled by mighty 'King' class locomotives, some non-stop through the station, and Southern Region trains requiring banking assistance to ascend the 1 in 30 incline to Central station, to a cacophony of sound from engine whistles! It has to be seen and heard to be believed!

Apart from two short trips in the mid-1950s referred to earlier, I don't become familiar with the 'withered arm' until May 1962, when I spend three days and travel almost the entire network. Motive power by now is either a 'West Country' light pacific or a 'Maunsell N class,' these tending to be on the far ends of the network. Ex-LMS 'Ivatt' tanks are to the fore on the Wadebridge-Bodmin North and Halwill-Torrington trains. The entire network is fascinating, passing through large areas of open country and moorland of light population (doubtless is a reason for subsequent closure).

The journey west from Exeter leaves St David's station heading east for a mile to Cowley Bridge Junction, where it veers north, and Yeoford is the first junction on a web of lines, eventually reaching five destinations in Devon and Cornwall. The line north to Barnstaple still exists and thrives though the lines north and west of there are closed. Yeoford to Okehampton has regular passenger services restored in November 2021. All lines to the north, west, and south of here are *'dead 'n gorn'* (sic), as they say in Devon. Okehampton, a small market town on the edge of Dartmoor, is in its heyday the operations hub of these lines, having a locomotive shed with a modest fleet of small locomotives. Padstow and Bude carriages are detached from the Plymouth train to run to Halwill Junction, and Bude carriages are detached again, the main train running onto Padstow, an interesting though expensive operating mode.

An 'N' class locomotive at the small terminus at Padstow.
Unlike other termini, this one is close to the town centre and harbour.

The Ilfracombe line hangs on until 1970; here in August 1968, a train from Exeter
arrives with a 'Warship' class diesel.

The main line to Plymouth crosses the impressive Meldon Viaduct shortly after Okehampton, then over open moorland to Tavistock from where it runs along the Tamar Valley to Plymouth North Road, trains coming from London arriving there from the west on a line parallel to the Western line from Cornwall to London before taking a full 180-degree curve to terminate in Friary station. The line from Bere Alston to Plymouth is still extant as the Gunnislake branch. I manage to get to Callington, though, to my regret, never to Plymouth Friary.

The last section of the line runs along the picturesque Camel estuary with its notorious 'Doom Bar,' a treacherous sandbank. Padstow station has just one platform, sidings, and goods yard.

I return now to Yeoford Junction and the line to Barnstaple and beyond, on which I travel rarely up to recent years. The line to Ilfracombe survives 'Beeching' and eventually closes in 1970. I am very fortunate to go all the way there in August 1968 on railway business with a 'Warship' class diesel, and what a sorry sight the terminus looks, remote and aloft from the town with rusting excursion sidings as a reminder of better days past.

I muse on what might have happened in a rational world where inter-regional jealousies are not a factor, that social benefits accruing from maintaining a healthy holiday business are applied. Why did Newquay survive when Padstow didn't? What do I think could have happened in this mythical, rational world? Ilfracombe and Exeter to Plymouth via Okehampton retained, and Padstow served from Bodmin Road/Parkway. There is some hope that the section from Okehampton to Bere Alston via Tavistock might make the national network again though probably not in my lifetime. *What to do about the Meldon Viaduct?*

The coast between Barnstaple and Ilfracombe is outstandingly scenic.
Croyde beach is one of the top surfing places in the UK.

Fascinating Journeys 3　　　　**The Magic of Cornwall**

In October 1992, a train from Liskeard is running alongside the spectacular lower Looe valley to the terminus in Looe.

My earliest visit to Cornwall is in August 1954 when we have a family holiday in Newquay. There is a snag for me; I am due to start grammar school ten days after we arrive at Newquay and must travel back early, escorted by my father and grandfather (Bristol being the handover point), which I reluctantly accept. To soften the blow, Dad takes me on a wonderful day out, first by bus to Padstow, then a train to Wadebridge hauled by an 'ex-LSWR T9' locomotive (not many remain, even then), changing to a branch train to Bodmin Road. Back on the main line, we travel to Chacewater, west of Truro, and change to a train to Newquay via Perranporth. Some journey, of which the branch line parts of the trip are all to disappear under the 'Beeching' cuts! Newquay is then a station of four platforms and is only really busy on Saturdays in the summer.

Two years later, it is a long-distance camping trip with the scouts when we travel to a campsite near Penzance. They could not have chosen a better site as the walk into town is above the station, viewed from a retaining wall on its north side. I bunk off occasionally and spend happy hours train watching! The journey there is an exciting all-night marathon, and at daylight, in St Austell, I see a lot of 'Western National' buses outside in the station forecourt. Co-ordination is endemic, and most Cornish stations have a sign *"to the National Buses."*

I visit the County many times, sometimes on holiday, sometimes on day trips (long ones, it's a long way from anywhere) or, more often, short or weekend breaks. In the present century, I've taken three main holidays, at St Ives, Looe, and Falmouth, as recently as 2019. Over time, I've visited virtually everywhere of note and travelled all railway lines still current and many of now closed. Only one gets away – Gwinear Road to Helston – and one which loses its passenger service – Lostwithiel to Fowey – I travel by freight train as part of a project on China Clay traffic.

Let me take you through a selection of my experiences on the following page.

An Cornish Railways Miscellany

Newquay in the mid- 1970s, reduced from four to three platforms and destined to be just a single platform ten years later. On this summer Saturday, a through train to London Paddington is waiting to leave as a local train from Par is arriving. By the late 1980s, locomotive haulage is no more as the run-round loop is taken out, and long-distance trains from London and elsewhere are 'Inter City 125's', with diesel railcars on local trains.

Fortunately, Penzance station survives intact, still with four platforms to the present day. This photograph, taken in 1987, shows a busy scene with an 'Intercity 125' on a London train and Class 47 diesel on a 'Cross-Country' train. The only real changes compared with 1956 (when I first see the view over the retaining wall) are those from steam

to diesel traction and the removal of quayside sidings. The modern scene includes 'Intercity Express (IET)' on London trains and 'Voyagers' on cross-country trains.

Cornish railways are happily seeing a renaissance in recent years, and the Falmouth branch gets a doubling of service after a new loop is installed at Penryn. To avoid building a second platform, the loop comes in halfway along an extended platform, as seen here. The Falmouth branch becomes easily the busiest all-year-round service in Cornwall. Apart from one summer Saturday train to Paddington up to the early 1960s, Falmouth has never had through mainline trains, and after steam ends, is operated entirely by diesel railcars.

St Ives Bay is noted for having the most amazing blue sea and St Ives itself
for its incredible beauty and arty ambiance.

Josiane and I take holidays in Cornwall several times in the present century. Our first to St Ives is by car, using trains and buses for outings in the week. On the other trips, we travel to Cornwall by train and hire a car for the week or so's holiday, doing some local journeys by car, usually where it's not possible or easy by train and seeing some places new to us. The main highlights are an open-top bus along the coast via Zennor and Land's End to Penzance, and a visit to the newly opened 'Eden Project' taking the train to St Austell then by special scheduled connecting bus. As we leave on the train from St Ives, there is a 'wow' factor looking across at what must be the most vivid blue water anywhere in Britain. All too soon, we are in St Erth and on the main line to St Austell. The Cornwall main line from Penzance to the Tamar is full of interest, from the fine scenery to the great history of the county on view interspersed with brief views of the sea. The 'Eden Centre' proves utterly fascinating and takes up a whole day.

Looe is our next holiday destination in 2014. In July, we travel by train to Plymouth (which we thought may not be possible following the Dawlish sea wall disaster in late 2013 but pass through unimpeded. We hire a car at Plymouth and reach Looe via the Torpoint ferry. We make a train journey to St Ives and a bus to nearby Polperro; also, to the 'Lost Gardens of Heligan,' a remarkable restoration project which I rate better than the 'Eden Project.' We travel to north Cornwall to visit Port Isaac (*Portwenn* in the *Doc Martin* TV series); thwarted by parking problems and rain coming down in stair rods, we divert to Rock, then back over Bodmin Moor. In 2019, we visit Falmouth for the first time and enjoy a week's unbroken sunshine and visit the fabulous St Mawes and Roseland Peninsula, as well as a train to Penzance and bus to Newlyn and Mousehole.

Exmoor National Park   **Steam and Sublimity**

The delightful Exmoor village of Exford.

My first introduction to Exmoor is in 1952. That year the family holiday is in Minehead, which is at the end of a long branch line from Taunton (now the heritage West Somerset Railway). My father, always exploring new travel ideas, takes us on the 'PS Cardiff Queen' from Minehead to Ilfracombe, incidentally, calling en route at Lynmouth just one month before the village is devastated in a calamitous flood. From Ilfracombe, we take a train to Barnstaple, changing to a Taunton-bound train to Dulverton. The station there is a mile above the small town and linked by a venerable 'Gilbern' bus, then by bus back to Minehead.

65 years later, Josiane and I spend a few days staying at Exford in the heart of Exmoor. My main objective is the West Somerset Railway, one of Britain's best heritage railways, but we see the Exmoor National Park as well. Three years later, we stay in Dunster, and one of our days out is to the 'Lynton & Barnstaple Railway,' all of one mile's sheer delight right in the

171

heart of the national park. Its station at Woody Bay (a misnomer, it's several miles from the real place on the coast). The 'L&B' closed in 1936, and we witness the start of big plans to restore this narrow-gauge line. A legend is encapsulated in that one mile, with locomotives and rolling stock beautifully restored and an atmosphere that is pure 1930s! That we spend all day there speaks volumes!

The classic photographic location near Woody Bay on the Lynton & Barnstaple Railway.

There is much more of Exmoor to explore, a countryside that is delightfully rural and rugged at the same time. I find that Dulverton is a small but important centre and the only 'town' in the interior of the national park. The winding road south from Dunster, much of it under tree arches, is most enchanting, and the Quantock Hills are omnipresent. The coastal road from Porlock to Lynton and Lynmouth reflects the topography with winding, steep hills and dire warnings to engage low gear! Lynmouth, a most attractive place rebuilt after the 1952 floods, is linked to Lynton on the hilltop by a cliff railway. Regrettably, it is too late in the day to use it, and you must take the eight-mile zig-zag road for the less than one mile near vertical climb!

Before leaving Exmoor, I must mention the West Somerset Railway on which I have travelled on and photographed enough times to make a book, let alone a chapter. Suffice to say that it is probably one of the most diverse and beautiful scenic lines with coast and country views in profusion. I have many photographs of steam trains on the line, mostly taken on gala days, and this one below ranks amongst my best.

Ex-GWR freight locomotive 3863 on a 'West Somerset Railway Gala' train at Washford. The scene conjures up images of summer Saturdays Minehead to London trains in the 1950s whose ten coaches needed a powerful locomotive.

Stroud Valley Autos — A Fascinating Rural Commuter Service

An auto train arrival from Gloucester at Chalford and will push its train back to Gloucester.

No, it's not the name of a local garage. It's the much more exciting story of the intensive service of one-or two-coach push-pull trains running between Gloucester and Chalford through the Stroud Valley.

I am drawn to this unique train service, the only one of its kind in the UK to my knowledge. The trains run roughly every hour throughout the working day, non-stop between Gloucester and Stonehouse (9 miles on fast mainline track), then ten stops up the valley to Chalford (7 miles). The plucky little tank engines with large driving wheels are known to hit 80 mph on the main line, and I personally record 72 mph as we race a Gloucester-Bristol stopping train on the parallel tracks of the ex-LMS line (and pull ahead of that train hauled by a larger 'Royal Scot' with just five coaches!). I visit several times Between 1962 and 1964, and in the latter year, its impending closure is announced. On one visit, I take the train to Stonehouse and walk the 7 miles to Chalford, photograph a train at each halt, and create an interesting record of these remarkable trains.

BR Standard class 4 75078 crossing Summerseat viaduct on the East Lancashire Railway.

The North is undoubtedly my favourite part of England, even more so than the Southwest, which has been in my sights since my youngest days. My first introduction to the north is in 1954 when I attend my first scout camp, a very exciting journey. Travelling overnight from Cardiff on the midnight train, arrival at Crewe is about 03:30 with a 3-hour wait for our train north. Crewe station has a retaining wall between north- and south-bound platforms, and most activity is beyond it (southbound Anglo-Scottish trains), except that I can't see them, and the leaders won't let me out of their sight. The next leg of the journey is by stopping train to Preston, which zigzags north of Warrington via Earlestown and Newton-le-Willows, and nearly all the way, it is four-tracked, something new to me. Preston is reached at nine, and I recall another long wait, but I can at least see all that's happening – and how! It is a Saturday morning, and traffic to and from Blackpool is in full flow; I have never seen so many trains in my life, and they're all steam-hauled! The journey on to Windermere is on a train hauled by an ex-LMS 'Fowler' tank locomotive.

The die is cast and reinforced 12 years later when I am working in Leeds. In the interim, I have a North Eastern Region 'Rail Rover' ticket in 1961 and travel over two amazing lines that close soon after, leaving an indelible memory: the Haltwhistle to Alston branch and Darlington to Penrith cross-country line, both through some of northern England's wildest country and over spectacular viaducts.

I have selected three railway lines and/or areas that interest me: the famous Settle & Carlisle, the Calder Valley Line and Oldham Loop, and finally, those circling the Lake District.

Travels in the Lancashire Cotton Belt

The Calder Valley and Oldham Loop

A Class 156 'Sprinter' passing Todmorden en route from Manchester to Bradford and Leeds.

My earliest introduction to Manchester and the railways north and north-east thereof is in early September 1959 when staying in Chester with a school friend and fellow enthusiast. We travel to Manchester and spend the day at the adjacent Victoria and Exchange stations, linked by England's longest platform; Exchange is in Salford, Victoria is in Manchester, very strange, I think! Most trains to the west are steam-hauled, but those to Bury are electric and those to Oldham and Rochdale, diesel, so I pay little attention to them. It's a fascinating place for train watching, and I find the most interesting sight is the two ex- 'Lancashire & Yorkshire Railway' locomotives on the middle track for banking heavy trains over the steep climb to Miles Platting to the east. There's not much work for them as we only see one banking operation in four hours!

A year or so later, I read a regular weekly article in the Manchester Guardian (nowadays 'The Guardian'), and an article of great interest comes up: *"See the Industrial Revolution as it was in 1760 on a train from Manchester to Rochdale via Oldham."* The writer is evidently fascinated by the number of old mills and other artefacts of that age still extant. In 1962, I spend a week with Hugh in Chester, and as a break from the North Wales and Cambrian lines, we travel into Lancashire on a rather wet day. It doesn't look at its best in these conditions, nevertheless, it's an interesting trip. First to Runcorn via the Halton curve (recently reopened), then Liverpool (Lime St & Exchange), on to Preston, and down to Bolton. It gets interesting when we board a cross-Lancashire train (Southport to Rochdale) through Radcliffe, Bury, Heywood, and Castleton, the heart of the cotton mill scene.

A westbound train at Manchester Victoria on a dull day in 1962.

Two 'Pacers' at Manchester Vic (the one at the rear is in a chocolate/white livery and recently transferred from Devon.

We are in a diesel railcar but notice other trains are steam hauled. It is subsequently a 'Beeching' closure, one I've never made sense of, as it links five of Lancashire's largest towns! At Rochdale, a chance to try the Oldham loop and see if it lives up to its 1760 billing! Our train is a feisty 'Cravens' diesel railcar with both cars powered to tackle the hard grades, and yes, the

industrial scene *is* utterly fascinating if more than a little run down, and we enjoy the trip

180

very much. Shaw & Crompton, the latter is quite likely the origin of *Crompton's Mule*; oddly named Oldham Mumps station and its signal boxes Mumps No. 1 & No.2, Newton Heath shed, full of steam engines, and finally the steep downhill run from Miles Platting to Victoria station in Manchester.

It's another four years before I'm back in Manchester Victoria, and the first thing I notice is (apart from the massive reduction in steam traction) that the station looks as run down as before (apparently, it was badly damaged during the war with only patch and mend). The trains are looking equally run down, and I wonder just how bad regular travelling is on this part of the railway. Things perk up when I join a train to Leeds via the Calder Valley; it is one of the powerful three-car Class 110 diesel railcars which give a very thrilling ride through the wonderful industrial, rugged landscapes, with more mills (cotton in Lancashire then woollen in Yorkshire). After Rochdale, the long climb to Summit Tunnel is taken with gusto, speed, and much noise from thrusting engines as we tear through the tunnel to drop down into Yorkshire via Todmorden, Hebden Bridge, and Sowerby Bridge. After that, it turns towards Halifax, another steep climb followed by a sharp down grade into Bradford and its gloomy Exchange station. I think I'm going to like this line!

In my 18 months of working in Leeds, I make frequent trans-Pennine journeys, most of them to Manchester via the former 'London & North Western' route via Standedge, but I return several times via the Calder Valley and find it the more interesting, if slower, of the two. Another line joins from Burnley but is then freight-only. On weekends in autumn, it hosts a special from Leeds to Blackpool for the famous Illuminations; it is steam hauled, and when I travel, it is hauled by a 'Jubilee' class locomotive. Its route from Leeds is via Dewsbury and Brighouse, then over Copy Pit summit, Blackburn, and Preston.

As to the Oldham Loop, my next trip is unusual and eventful. I'm on one of a series of 'end of British Rail steam' runs in August 1968, which leaves Manchester double-headed routed via the Oldham Loop. It seems the engineers haven't been told, and near Oldham, we are stopped for a long time whilst workers put the track back in front of us – red faces all round!

The train is to continue to Bolton, Blackburn, Colne, and Skipton, returning via Hellifield, Clitheroe, Blackburn, Lostock Hall, and Bolton, thence to Manchester.

I have always found this mid-Pennine landscape fascinating, a mixture of rugged mountains and hills with a (then) mostly thriving industrial scene. Even these days, with most industries gone, I still get a thrill travelling these lines. My trips over the Calder Valley continue sporadically in subsequent years but with a lot less excitement with 'Sprinter' trains and finally with 'Express' Class 158s. The scenery remains as exciting as ever, though with each passing year, a bit more history is erased. I return to the Oldham Loop several times on 'Pacer' trains; the same observations about its history pertain. On my 1991 trip, I recognise the train guard who I have seen at railway guards training classes at Cheltenham, where he is one of the lecturers when not working trains. Enquiring as to why he isn't issuing tickets, I am amazed as he tells me he is there to *"ring the bell and operate the doors"* as Greater Manchester Transport Authority is funding assistant ticket examiners (two per train) in a job creation scheme and he is forbidden from issuing tickets; three staff doing the job of one, a socialist nirvana!

The final chapter in this fascinating story is that my three most recent visits are by tram on a rejuvenated 'Manchester Metrolink' takeover, which takes the line for the first time through the streets of Oldham and to the town centre of Rochdale; and it looks good too, though there is a lot less industrial archaeology about.

2014 and 'Metrolink' trams are running through a lively Oldham Town Centre.
end of with Bury electric train and Oldham line Pacer in background.

My Impressions of the Famous Settle and Carlisle Line

The famous Ribblehead Viaduct is crossed by a special train with a rare visitor on the front, 'Bulleid' Pacific 34092.

There is nothing new I can add to the story of the Settle and Carlisle line, so I won't. Instead, I describe my impressions of a long and interesting association with the Line, which manifests itself in many and varied ways. Starting with my first journey from Leeds to Carlisle in 1961, through frequent trips and some lineside photography in my 18-month period working in Leeds in the mid to late 1960s; occasional trips with Peter when I visit him at his then Teesside home, and we drive over for photographic sessions; and finally on a number of diverted Sunday Glasgow to London trains between Carlisle and Preston; and more recent trips and observations.

In the summer of 1961, I take out a 7-day North Eastern Region 'Rail Rover', and my first use of the ticket is the 'Thames-Clyde Express' between Leeds and Carlisle hauled by a 'Royal Scot' class locomotive. Five years later living in Leeds, both summers there include trips on the infamous summer Saturday Sheffield to Glasgow reliefs. Once or twice, I use the sparse local service operated with diesel railcars to seek good photographic locations. Steam operation, though, is on borrowed time, and I and many others are shocked when, early in 1967, the 'Yorkshire Post' carries a stark headline to the effect that the Leeds-Carlisle line along with the local lines from Leeds/Bradford to Skipton/Ilkley are to be closed in 1970. This is so direct that it seems a decision has already been made by the British Railways Board as a *fait accompli*. The seeds are sown for a titanic struggle to keep the lines open. In the event, that closure doesn't happen though, things get very close in the mid-1980s.

In 1966/67, when I make local journeys to the Settle and Carlisle line, I will likely catch a local stopping train from Leeds to Skipton and connect to one of the thrice-daily all-stations trains from there to Carlisle. On this occasion (left), I alight at Settle station and walk to Settle Junction, where the S&C and the line onto Lancaster and Carnforth diverge. This way, I spend an afternoon photographing the remaining steam relief trains and some freight trains, many of which are still steam-hauled.

Sheffield-Glasgow relief at Skipton in late July 1967. 45562 *Alberta* hauls it from Leeds Whitehall to Carlisle.

It is fortunate that in the summers of 1966 and 1967, there is a rump of steam operation extant, mainly on freight services which are still quite plentiful even over this very difficult line. Steam passenger train services are confined to Saturdays in the summer, whereupon two long-distance trains each way have booked reliefs. The most famous, or as it turns out, infamous, is the relief to the 'Thames-Clyde Express' from Sheffield to Glasgow. Whereas these trains are habitually in and out of Leeds City, where reversal and locomotive changeover is effected, this in 1967 operates over the avoiding line at Whitehall Junction where locomotives and train crew change over. North of Leeds, it is hauled by one of Leeds Holbeck's five well-turned-out 'Jubilees,' and I ride behind *Alberta* and *Bengal*. Its infamy is down to the 'bush telegraph,' which suggests that it is feasible (though not permitted) to join the train here from trackside, and to my shame, I join in the fun. A travelling ticket inspector is present who takes a lot of money from this multitude of passengers, especially as he charges the fare from Sheffield, given the train doesn't officially call at Leeds.

7029 *Clun Castle* powering north through Kirkstall.

Not long before I leave Leeds, an interesting event on the 'S&C' is the visit of ex-GWR *Clun Castle,* which carries out some gauging tests prior to its hauling an excursion in mid-September 1967. On a rather wet morning, I cycle over to Kirkstall and manage a cracking shot of the northbound special. I hear the locomotive acquits itself quite well on this very punishing route to Carlisle. It is to be another ten years before I make more journeys over this line. The Sunday Anglo-Scottish trains, diverted on this route due to engineering work on the West Coast Main Line, run on the 'S&C' from Carlisle to Hellifield, then via Blackburn to reach the WCML at Preston. The locomotive, a Class 47, runs through from Glasgow to Preston.

46229 *Duchess of Sutherland* passing Culgaith in 1982

On three occasions, we return from rugby weekends in Scotland with the luxury of a fine lunch passing through the fells. On the first, we enjoy a winter wonderland of snow; on the third, the restaurant car is replaced by a buffet, and we cajole the stewardess to raid the fridge to serve us gammon and chips!

The next phase in my association with the Settle and Carlisle is a series of weekend visits by car. I stay with Peter in Yarm, and we travel to sample different parts of the route each time. I rate all parts north of Skipton equally for scenery and photographic locations though my best shots are in places like Culgaith, north of Appleby, or leaving Garsdale heading south with the famous 'Flying Scotsman.'

On one memorable occasion, Peter and I join a special train at Middlesborough, which travels via the Durham Coast Line and Newcastle to Carlisle. It's a cold and icy day, we have A4 Pacific

Sir Nigel Gresley from Carlisle to Leeds, and a photo/water stop is arranged at Garsdale. It's very cold as we take shots of the standing train. Since the mid-1980s, I make only sporadic trips to the line, on one occasion, spending the night in the station house at Settle. This, at the time of massive new coal traffic flows from the port of Hunterston to English power stations and I can hardly sleep due to the all-night rumble of passing trains. I make two trips, one over the whole line with a 'Sprinter' diesel railcar, the other with a 'Pacer' railbus, inappropriate motive power for a line such as this. I realise that Northern Trains and its predecessors don't appear to appreciate the importance of providing a good travel experience to the many visitors.

On a bitterly cold day in February 1980, the southbound 'Cumbrian Mountain Express'
stands at Garsdale

The Cumbrian Fells and Coast and The Lake District

Coniston Water in December.

The Lake District, and Windermere in particular, is my first proper introduction to the North of England. Of the railways in the area, that from Oxenholme to Windermere is my most travelled route if I exclude the West Coast Main Line between Carnforth and Carlisle. As noted earlier in this chapter, I travel to Penrith from Darlington in 1961 and have enough time to slip down to Keswick and back; oh, that I could have gone through to Workington had the line not closed about ten years later! This only leaves the coastline on which I travel the entire 3-hour journey just once, though I make several journeys on the section from Carnforth to Barrow in Furness. One of these is on a special train from Leeds to Ravenglass in May 1966, which is hauled as far as Carnforth by restored ex-LNER *The Great Marquess,* then a 'Black Five' to Ravenglass over the Barrow avoiding line. The trip on the narrow-gauge 'Ravenglass and Eskdale' line completes a great day out. I travel the R&ER once more on 2nd May 1982. I recall the date well as the previous day, driving over the Hardknott Pass, I get news on the car radio of the infamous sinking of the 'General Belgrano' in the Falklands War!!

Oxenholme-Windermere

Summer evening in Windermere; a return excursion and a local service to Oxenholme.

I have four recorded years when I travel over this line; 1954, 1964, 1970, and 1989. Trips to Windermere after that are by car though I sometimes call in to look over the station, which by the turn of the century is just a single platform with a shuttle service from Oxenholme. On my first two visits, it is 100% steam with a variety of motive power, mostly tank locomotives of the ex-LMS 'Fowler' and 'Stanier' types. I find it busy in summer and, adding to the local trains which start variously at Lancaster, Carnforth, and Preston, additional through trains including a portion of the 'Lakes Express' from London Euston. In my 1964 visit, it's near the end for steam, and I am pleased to see a 'Britannia' at the head of a return excursion to somewhere in Lancashire. It's ripe for a great photograph, but the sun stays in until the very last moment, and then I get a beautiful shot. It's sad to see such a line below its potential due to excessive rationalisation. Nevertheless, in recent years, there are several through trains a day from Manchester though some are phased out gradually. A sign that it's still a force for encouraging active travel is the large bike hire centre at the station.

Lake Windermere has been famous for its steamers; four ships, the *Swan*, *Swift*, *Teal*, and *Tern* have been plying the lake for as long as I can remember. First introduced by the LMS Railway

'M.V. Teal' at Bowness in 1994, then 58 years young!

in 1936, the *Teal* is the oldest, but all the fleet is pre-war though rebuilt over the years. I make my first trip in 1954 (Chapter 7) and subsequently in 1994, on a short break after Christmas, when Josiane and I take a trip on *Teal* from Bowness Pier for an afternoon in Ambleside and enjoy its magical delights festooned with Christmas cheer.

At the lower end of the lake on its west shore is Lakeside station which I first see in 1954 with three steam trains are present. The line from Ulverston closes in the mid-1960s and is to reopen from Haverthwaite to Lake Side some years later to create a picturesque heritage line; however, in my case, seen but not travelled. Well, there is still time!

The Furness and Cumbrian Coast Lines

A 'Black Five' departing Barrow in Furness for Manchester.

The special train from Leeds referred to earlier is my first trip to the Furness region and the lower part of the Cumbrian Coast route. The destination is Ravenglass for the narrow-gauge route up Eskdale. It's a ten-mile trip that takes us into the wild western Lakeland Fells, a most interesting day out.

It is to be another sixteen years before I reach the west coast again, staying the night at Ravenglass before another trip up Eskdale. There is, of course, much more to the Cumbrian Coast Line as I am to find out in 1989 when I opt to travel from Carlisle to Preston, a four and a half hour journey this way, compared to just under an hour on the WCML. It is a most interesting journey in a diesel railcar. I discover a post and present industrial landscape all the way along and a coastline very similar in many ways to the Cambrian. The north end is littered with remains of mining and steel making, with one steel plant at Workington still extant. Then, to my surprise, the sheer scale of the Sellafield nuclear complex halfway down the line is still very much alive to the present day and provides lots of passengers and some freight in and out of its sprawling site. It's post-industrial again at Millom, and at Barrow, there's a mix of previous – and declining present-day – industrial activity. Once along the shores of Morecambe Bay, the industry disappears except for the sight of the Heysham nuclear power plant across the water.

One more visit early in the present century sees me at a 'Community Rail' conference at Grange over Sands. Organiser Paul Salveson – always one for a great event and post-event – arranges for us to dine at a pub in Arnside across the Kent Estuary, returning on the last train. He hasn't confirmed to the landlord that around 40 meals are required in just two hours, and it is touch and go for our train back; but again, he falls on his feet, and we enjoy a superb evening out!

I go several times with Josiane between Christmas and New Year in the late 1990s, staying at a smart Bowness hotel offering big discounts, but these are road trips apart from the lake steamer mentioned above. I discover the magic of the gorgeous Lake District towns of Ambleside and Keswick, beautifully lit up and decorated for the festive season, well worth the long drive to and from South Wales.

One amusing aside is when I take Josiane to Little Langdale and revisit the 'Old Dungeon Ghyll' inn, where I spent many happy hours, mainly in the 1960s and 70s. Always there, either soaking wet or with thick, muddy boots on, I ask the landlord whether he will serve us, wearing smart clothing. Reverse discrimination, and he is happy to make us welcome as a former regular!

Chapter 12

A Tale of Three Cities:

Leeds, Bristol, and Norwich

In an average railway management career, it's a given that one will face frequent promotions, many of them involving relocating to distant parts of the country. In this respect, I am among the exceptions, with jobs in only three parts of England, and the greater part of my career is spent in Wales.

It's early 1966, five years into my railway career, when I make my first big move, by choice, to distant Leeds, and whilst the work isn't to my satisfaction, it opens completely new horizons for me. My next big city move is partly choice, partly persuasion as I opt for the West of England Division for management training and Bristol as my principal base for a living (though I spend periods in Worcester, Plymouth, and London).

Looking for a change after eight years in freight sales and marketing and several job interviews which could have seen me in Liverpool, Newcastle, and Glasgow, I become Passenger Sales and Marketing Manager for East Anglia, based in Norwich, where I spend almost four years.

I have always believed in the value of 'going native' when moving, immersing myself in both the culture and life of my chosen location, and in this chapter, I relate my impressions of three English cities from this perspective as well as commentary on the prevailing transport scene.

There are lots of interesting English cities where I spend varying amounts of time, but there are only three others that I know reasonably well. Top of the list is York, where I attend many conferences over the years with some free time to look over the city's many attractions. Manchester and Birmingham take equal billing as I stay in both for short periods several times.

York

My first visit is 1961 when I spend a summer Saturday there amazed at the sheer variety of trains, mostly steam with some local diesel railcars. The highlight for me are the A4 Pacific's – known to the spotters as *'streaks'* – the mainstay of Anglo-Scottish trains. During my time at Leeds, I visit York frequently, and in later years, it is the location for annual conferences of 'Community Railways' in the National Railway Museum. I am often accompanied by Josiane, and we enjoy the unique atmosphere of this incredibly historic and fascinating city.

Manchester

A city visited for its transport interest though I enjoy its many attractions, recently the iconic Salford Quays and L S Lowry Museum. An attraction is the rapidly expanding Metrolink tram system, whose growth I follow from its inception in the 1990s. Its two large rail termini as different as chalk and cheese; sleek and efficient Piccadilly to formerly run down the (and currently little better) replacement of Victoria.

Birmingham

A great railway hub that I get to know in the latter half of the 1950s. Its two main stations are New Street, dark, noisy, and dirty, and Snow Hill, which is well laid out with a relaxed air. The latter closes in the mid-60s, and its trains transferred to New Street or Moor Street. New Street is rebuilt as a soul-destroying concrete jungle. I love the old Snow Hill with its well-ordered steam-operated suburban trains and expresses to Paddington hauled by the famous 'King' class locos. By the present century, pride and sense have returned with a rebuilt New Street and Grand Central development; and a reopened but much smaller utility-style Snow Hill and trams have returned to the streets again.

Leeds — Commercial Heart of West Yorkshire

Leeds Town Hall, a monument to the Victorian enterprise.

I move to Leeds in the early spring of 1966 to start a new job and experience living in a large city for the first time in my life. After a 6-hour journey from Neath, changing at Gloucester, and a frustratingly slow train, especially north of Sheffield, I arrive with my bike and head to a pre-arranged guest house just north of the city centre. As I juggle a bike and luggage on a traffic island, the heavens open, and I arrive at my lodgings soaking wet and tired. Apart from the job (Chapter 7), it all gets better from then on.

First impressions

A great welcome from local folk; heavy traffic and awful fumes; a large and busy train station; and a fascinating city somewhat degraded by insensitive development but with some notable features – such as a majestic, blackened town hall; 'Whitelock's' pub with great ale, Yorkshire puddings, and waitresses in frilly dresses; brass band lunchtime recitals – to name but a few. After a week, I move into 'digs' run by a fearsome landlady and share a room with two Yorkshire 'blokes' who put me through 'rookie' rituals. It's in Headingly, close to the cricket ground and railway station (with a poor service for a city suburban line) so I use the bus. Each evening I pass a pub called 'The Skyrack', a name which has puzzled me until now (Colin Speakman, in his latest book *Yorkshire* explains it's the name given to an ancient oak tree, a place where local disputes were settled in days of rule by Norsemen). After two months, I move to a small furnished flat in leafy Bramhope, commuting mainly on a 'Ledgard's' bus, but sometimes having a lift from friends to Horsforth station, and stay there until I move on later in 1967.

I relate in Chapter 7 about my interesting outdoor life, though spend a lot of time in the city, Otley and Wharfedale, enjoy fish and chips from the original 'Harry Ramsden's' at Guiseley (two bus journeys changing at Otley, quite something to get to a chippie!). Otley is my local town, reputed to hold the English record for pubs per head of population; it has a train station when I first stay there in 1961, but it is gone a few years later. Leeds is a handsome city with an interesting centre of narrow streets within a grid formed by Briggate, Boar Lane, and The Headrow, some lovely arcades with a good cultural life.

The famous 'Whitelock's' lunch bar, a Leeds institution (*Colin Speakman*).

Public transport in Leeds is at the time, good in parts, but not what I expect in a large regional city. The ubiquitous two-tone green city buses are everywhere, but regional bus services by numerous operators (West Riding, Yorkshire Woollen District, Yorkshire Traction), to name a few, are exiled to a nondescript bus station on the eastern edge of the city. My route out to Bramhope is operated by 'Ledgard's' with some journeys by 'West Yorkshire' (who took them over in mid-1967).

Leeds City station in 1967, ugly, rambling, busy with trains and people.

The railway scene is interesting with all trains using a newly rebuilt but utilitarian City station though the passenger entrance is still via the magnificent Wellington concourse, which has a few terminating platforms. At its far end was Central station which closed several years earlier. Most of the remaining lines from Leeds are to the north-west, west, and south-west of the city, and the west end layout is complex. There is just one line to the east, creating a bottleneck as it is also the access to a massive Neville Hill depot; this line divides further east into lines to Selby and Hull, and to York and Newcastle.

In 1966/67, there are still two London termini served direct from Leeds: King's Cross (the main route) and St Pancras. Other inter-city style services go south to Sheffield and beyond, the trans Pennine route across to Manchester via Huddersfield, which is operated by new and stylish 'Trans Pennine' diesel trains and several through Liverpool-Newcastle locomotive-hauled trains. The latter reverse at Leeds, the route to Harrogate via Wetherby having been shut, and now they take the route via Horsforth, Harrogate, and Ripon.

Local services are a declining species with frequent trains to Bradford and the Calder Valley, less frequent to Bradford Forster Square, Skipton, and Ilkley (and these, along with the Settle & Carlisle, are threatened with complete closure by 1970). Despite this, it is a very busy and interesting station, still with a smattering of steam haulage.

My more recent occasional visits see a transformed and much larger Leeds City, but even this has difficulty coping with exponential growth in traffic.

Leeds City station 2004, bigger, better and busier than in 1967.

Bristol	A Great Maritime City

Panoramic view of Bristol city from the harbour, A cathedral in the foreground, university, and Wills Memorial Tower (background).

The magnificent St Mary Redcliffe church spire.

I arrive in Bristol less than six months after leaving Leeds, as a British Rail management trainee based in its West of England Division. After spending a few months in Worcester, I domicile myself in the city for the remainder of the two-year course. Though not much smaller than Leeds, I find Bristol is a very different city with a laid-back style and less cut and thrust than I have been accustomed to. That is to change markedly in later years as it re-establishes itself as a modern city. One thing it has in common with Leeds is an aspiration to be a city based on motorways and cars, a policy that will (and does) lead to disastrous congestion in later years.

The waterfront of the late 60s is in heavy and terminal decline as its commercial role ceases; it takes years to reverse that and create a truly modern and exciting feature. The old Bristol that survives the *'blitz'* creates a lovely historic centre surrounded by mediocre, tasteless modern development. In the middle of all this is a very vibrant cultural scene, and I am introduced to modern classical music and theatre and great nightlife. The 'Bohemian' Clifton Village is at the heart of Bristol's architectural splendours, including the iconic Suspension Bridge which I had visited as a child.

In subsequent years' visits, I watch its transformation into a modern and stylish metropolis. My most recent staying visit coincides with the infamous 'beast from the east.' Even so, Josiane and I manage to both walk and drive over an iced-up Clifton Bridge and enjoy a great lunch in the warmth of a lovely café.

Bristol Temple Meads' neo-Gothic architecture and fine overall roof are a transport delight.

In public transport terms, Bristol in the late 1960s is an even worse situation than Leeds. Part of the reason is in the siting of its principal station, Temple Meads, a good half-mile or more from the city centre, with a very circuitous suburban railway. However, its bus services are not a lot better, and sadly, reliability is poor, and there appears to be a permanent war between bus crews and passengers, hardly an advertisement for a good service!

For over a year, I share a flat with three others in Bishopston, two miles north of the city. I despair of the bus service and take to the train by walking half a mile to Montpelier station for a four-mile circuit to Temple Meads. My morning train is a single diesel railcar with a handful of passengers, surely destined for closure. Happily, 55 years on, trains there are thriving with a half-hourly service all day!

Temple Meads is a station in the grand style, with its neo-Gothic entrance and wonderful overall roof. It is also very interesting operationally, and I learn much about the management of a large station. However, I discover the Bristol laid-back style when frequently my questions are answered with *"Well, it's all accordin', see!"* I undertake some very interesting projects, including one investigating the effects of closing the Temple Meads avoiding lines used by freight trains. This involves me spending five night shifts at the station, where I learn about the massive but unseen security operation (post 'Great Train Robbery') to ensure the safe passage of £2 million worth of post that passes through this hub each night (and £2m was an awful lot of money then!). In the intervening years, I visit the station many times and delight in witnessing its increasing prosperity.

'Bristol Omnibus' buses in the late 1960s.

Norwich	A Fine City

A late afternoon winter view of Norwich looking from Rackheath.

A fine city with a fine cathedral.

I only discover the meaning of the suffix 'A Fine City' on the road signs when it is explained by comedian *Mike Yarwood* at the Theatre Royal after being issued with a parking ticket!

However, as the third city in England where I live, I find it's a most elegant, interesting place with a fine cathedral, vying with Salisbury for its lofty spire. As observed in chapter 7, the area is mainly flat but has some significant hilly parts, as I discover after unwisely opting for a 1100cc new car on arrival.

Norwich is a most liveable city with its lovely Elm Hill area as well as many other historic buildings. The Georgian 'Assembly House' is a great place to unwind with afternoon tea after a hard day in the office. I also enjoy patronising its lively 'Theatre Royal', at the time boasting a programme on 364 days/year; amazingly, it attracts famous comedian *Max Boyce* with his very Welsh (and rugby) brand of humour for three years running, playing to packed houses each time!

My working territory extends over East Anglia to Cambridge and Ipswich, amongst other places, so I get the experience of an unfamiliar (to me) flat landscape though, in my leisure time, I warm to two areas that become special to me, the wild North Norfolk seascape, and the gentler East Suffolk coast; whilst I also find inland Suffolk particularly attractive with its picturesque villages. A downside to Norwich in the early 1980s is that it has become a beer desert, with (to my taste) a particularly awful brew from local Norwich Brewery! This leads to a quest to find some decent real ale alternatives which are found by hard detective work: Adnam's of Southwold, Greene King of Bury St Edmunds, and Tolly Cobbold of Ipswich.

The frozen River Wensum at Norwich in Winter 1981.

My work colleagues warn me when I get there in late 1979 that the winters are bitterly cold though it is not until the 1981 season that I experience one. In that year, it is so cold that the river Wensum flowing through the city freezes solid. I organise a train trip to York pre-Christmas using a classic 'Deltic' locomotive and fill all 13 coaches; unfortunately, ice in the steam pipes leaves the last five coaches unheated and lots of passenger complaints to deal with!

Otherwise, the transport scene in Norwich is very interesting though, it must be said, pretty run down as well. The East Anglian area it seems is not deemed important enough for major investment with local trains run with 25-year-old diesel railcars, and the main line to London uses second-hand intercity coaches. There is a network of four busy local routes out of the city

A busy scene at Norwich Thorpe station.

through quite scenic areas, and I am particularly fond of the line to Sheringham on the North Norfolk coast; there are also routes to Great Yarmouth, Lowestoft, and Ely, all very busy.

Bus services in Norwich City are generally good though I must confess I rarely use them; my route from Taverham has only an hourly service even in the peak. Rural services from the city are sparse and appear to be in a terminal decline. In my role as a rail marketing person, though in competition with buses for local traffic, I maintain cordial relations with the Eastern Counties bus company, even to the extent of getting unofficial driving lessons outside working hours on a 'Bristol Lodekka' to try and get a PSV licence. As I move on promotion to Cardiff, it is time to apply for the licence. Therefore I still can't drive a bus!

One big difference between Norwich and both Bristol and Leeds is that there is no motorway or a prospect of one (though I'm sure they would like one), so standard roads and congestion are the order of the day. Norwich pioneers the first network of traffic lights at roundabouts on the ring road, which brings traffic to gridlock when introduced and is postponed for several years. The city is jinxed as the brand-new Crown Point train servicing depot is gridlocked on opening in late 1982 when it takes a whole morning before trains move out!

In the following two pages, I describe my chance encounter with the London, Tilbury, and Southend line in its dying years of operation by steam traction. It is instantly fascinating because it is so different as a stand-alone commuter network almost completely divorced from the main railway and is operated very efficiently using motive power and rolling stock well past its sell-by date.

Whilst in London for a week at a time two years running in the late 1950s, I take the opportunity to look at the other termini still largely operated by steam traction. These include Paddington, Euston, St Pancras, and Liverpool Street. The interesting thing is that all these termini are about to see a transformation in motive power and operations though one does not see very much about the future – except for the Eastern Region, which has Liverpool Street and Fenchurch Street station termini. Both are to see a metamorphosis over the following years into electrification and the Region mounts a competition and project to be a 'progress chaser,' aimed at enthusing young people like myself (and many of us are 'steam enthusiasts') to embrace a completely new style of railway operation.

Unlike many parts of the railway, the Eastern Region has been quietly modernising many practises even while steam and, later, diesel, operation is endemic. Thus, for many years, not only the L T & S but also the Liverpool Street to Chingford and Enfield Town services are running at five minutes frequency over two lines of track out of the termini; and using just four platforms at each terminus. That from Liverpool Street is known as the 'Jazz' a name that goes back many years and is synonymous with highly efficient operation. The trains, all hauled by ex-LNER 'N7' tank locomotives, are recognised instantly at the buffer stops by the distinctive sound of their Westinghouse air brakes. Travelling on these trains, formed of quad-articulated rakes of carriages, is slow with frequent stops: Bethnal Green, Cambridge Heath, London Fields, Hackney Downs, Clapton, then three Walthamstow stations, St James

Street, Hoe Street, and Wood Street (where the locomotive sheds are); finally, Highams Park and leafy Chingford. Today, one would hardly recognise Bethnal Green and Hackney, which have become gentrified.

In my two weeks there in the late fifties, I come to like the East End and its people, many of whom have come through dramatic times, first with the 'blitz' and later with the massive closures of the docks and associated industries.

An East End Wonder   The London, Tilbury and Southend Railway

1962 and final year of steam on the LT&S.
A train from Southend arriving and locomotive in headshunt (background).

Battle of Cable Street, Stepney, 1936 *(Mervyn Mitton).*

Many of life's experiences stem from chance encounters. One of these is my association, followed by real enthusiasm, for the steam-operated railway running through London's East End. I return from my first foreign holiday in late July 1958 before my parents get back from theirs. So, at London's Victoria station, I head east instead of west to stay in Roland House, a Scout Association hostel in Stepney, arriving at Stepney Green underground station and head to the hostel through dark narrow streets, which is not an ideal situation. The next morning, I set out to find the main line station at Stepney East (it is now known as Limehouse) and come across Cable Street of which I learn from history lessons as the 'Battle of Cable Street' in 1936 when the Oswald Mosley fascists have a very bitter affray with the police. The area has dark associations with 'Jack the Ripper' in nearby Whitechapel and, at the time, the Kray Brothers are about their dirty work. Blimey! I find that Stepney East has 100% steam service on the London, Tilbury & Southend line. So first, I go into Fenchurch Street, the lines' small terminus, just four platforms elevated above street level and not blessed with an 'Underground' connection.

My fascination with this 60-mile system (which stretches east to Tilbury, Southend, and Shoeburyness) starts with my watching with utter fascination that day's evening peak operation. Twelve trains an hour, each of 8 to 12 coaches hauled by a steam locomotive, leaving at five-minute intervals on the line out to Barking. Each set of coaches must be in and out in 20 minutes, the locomotive released into a headshunt, reversing back into the station to head the next departure, and so on, and everything seems to run to time!

In the following year, 1959, an identical situation arises with my returning from France, my parents still on holiday, so I am back for another week in Stepney. By the end of my week there, I travel over the entire system, all steam hauled, and become aware of how it is kept going on a wing and prayer and professional operation. Electrification masts appear, and the steam locomotives are all marking time, getting steadily older and dirtier. The fleet of 'Stanier-built' three-cylinder tanks (more powerful than the other 'Stanier' tanks) are in a run-down state, and BR Standard Class 4 (80xxx series) are replacing them, also looking careworn. Whilst the situation at Fenchurch Street remains impressive, I become full of admiration at how lively these tank locomotives are on their 12 coach trains with frequent stops.

In the summer of 1960, I read that the employment situation is so desperate at Plaistow depot in east London that they are advertising summer jobs for engine cleaners with prospects as 'passed firemen,' so I apply, knowing I will be able to lodge cheaply in Stepney, not too far from the depot. As soon as my mother hears of this, it puts the kibosh on things, so I never take up the offer; I wish I had been more rebellious then!

Another 1962 view of Fenchurch Street looking towards the city.

I go back on a day trip in September 1962, by now armed with my first colour slide camera, and take several shots of what is to be the final year of steam. Thereafter, I virtually lose touch with the line until 1997. I am engaged in a consultancy study for Silverlink Trains on the Gospel Oak-Barking line, which is then suffering from dreadful service with clapped-out diesel multiple units. I think a future option to be an extension of service beyond Barking to Grays via Upminster to serve the giant Lakeside Shopping Mall near Chafford Hundred station; however, it doesn't look like a good proposition. I travel from Fenchurch Street on new electric multiple units, but there's no atmosphere.

My final look at the LT&S is in 2013 when I travel the entire Docklands Light Railway and Emirates Air Line and get a landward and bird's eye view of the system. I alight at the DLR Limehouse station and transfer across to the erstwhile Stepney East for a nostalgic trip into Fenchurch Street.

GLOSSARY OF TERMS

Rail Transport

Auto train: A push-pull train with a locomotive at one end and a control cab at the other.

Beeching (Dr), was brought in to overhaul British Rail's finances in 1963.

Black Five: Generic name given to a class of mixed traffic locomotives of the LMS.

Blue trains: Bright new electric trains for the north Clyde network in 1960.

BRCW/North British/Sulzer: Various types of small diesel locomotives in Scotland.

BR Standard locomotives: A series of steam locomotive types introduced from 1951 to 1960.

Britannia: A class of 55 express steam locomotives introduced in 1951.

Bulleid Pacific: 'Streamlined' Southern Railway express steam locomotive designed by O.V.S. Bulleid.

Castle: A class of over 150 GWR express steam locomotives introduced in the 1920s.

Class 47 diesel: The ubiquitous mixed traffic diesel locomotive built by Sulzer.

Crab: Generic name given to small ex-LMS tender locomotives.

Cravens/Derby LW/Metro Cammell: Three types of first-generation diesel railcars.

Crompton diesel: Another mixed traffic diesel locomotive, otherwise known as the 'Peak' class.

DART: Dublin Area Rapid Transit, suburban train services around the city.

EE or English Electric type 3: A ubiquitous mid-powered diesel locomotive.

Flying Scotsman: Probably the most famous but not the fastest steam locomotive

GWR: Great Western Railway, absorbed into British Railways in 1948.

Hymek: A medium-powered diesel-hydraulic locomotive in the Western Region.

Iarnrod Eireann (IE): Irish republic national railway.

Inter City 125: A high-speed diesel train introduced in 1975 for main non-electrified lines.

King: A class of 30 GWR super express steam locomotives introduced in the 1930s.

L&YR: Lancashire & Yorkshire railway, a constituent of the LMS prior to 1921.

LMS: London, Midland, and Scottish Railway, absorbed into British Railways in 1948.

LNWR: London & North Western Railway, a constituent of the LMS prior to 1921.

LSWR: London and South Western Railway, a constituent of the Southern Railway prior to 1921.

Manor: A class of 30 GWR steam locomotives for secondary main lines.

Midland Railway: A constituent of the LMS prior to 1921.

Northern Ireland Railways (NIR): National railway in the North of Ireland.

Pacer: A four-wheeled railbus based on the Leyland National bus.

(Princess) Coronation: Given name of top-rank locomotives used on Anglo-Scottish trains up to the early 1960s.

Settle and Carlisle Line: Name given to iconic route over the Pennines north of Leeds.

Sleeper: Sleeping car service train.

SLOA: Steam locomotive operators association.

Sprinter: Second-generation diesel railcars introduced nationally in 1985.

Warship: A higher-powered diesel-hydraulic locomotive on the Western Region, all named after warships.

Other Transport

Arriva: Name given to one of the largest bus and rail groups in the UK.

Bus Eireann: Cross country and express buses in the Republic.

Citybus: Belfast city bus services.

Gower Explorer: The generic name bestowed on the revamped Gower bus service in 2004.

Lodekka and K type: Marques of double-decker buses of the 1950s & 1960s

Mumbles train: The Swansea & Mumbles Railway, run by double-deck tramcars and closed in 1960.

M.V.: Shorthand for Motor Vessel.

P.S.: Shorthand for Paddle Steamer.

Snowdon Sherpa: A comprehensive network of buses in the Snowdonia National Park.

Stagecoach: Name given to one of the largest bus and rail groups in the UK.

Traws Cambria: The original name for a handful of north-south Wales express buses.

Traws Cymru: Present-day development of Traws Cambria, a network of express buses across rural Wales.

T.S.: Shorthand for Turbine-driven steamer

Ulsterbus: General bus services throughout Northern Ireland

General

BMI Baby: Low-cost carrier spin-off from British Midland Airways.

Butlin's: Family holiday camps situated over the British Isles.

Dylan Thomas: A famous Welsh bard and poet (1914-53), lived in Swansea.

Gaelic: The national language of Ireland.

Hornby: A model railway company set up in the 1950s by Frank Hornby.

IRA: Irish Republican Army.

Munro: Name bestowed on mountains of over 3000 feet by one who climbed them all.

Mynydd: Welsh name for mountain.

Scwd: Welsh name for waterfall or cascade.

Sunderland Flying Boats: Second World War amphibious aircraft based at Pembroke Dock.

The first Severn Bridge (Lydney-Sharpness): Predating the extant Severn crossings by over 100 years.

The Troubles: Name given to the 'civil war' in Northern Ireland in the late 20th Century.

Lightning Source UK Ltd.
Milton Keynes UK
UKHW021430031222
413207UK00006B/69